"Developing the habit of being continually aware of God's presence in your life is vital to reducing pressure and increasing personal peace in your heart. This valuable new book by Vance Pitman will show you the path to replacing stress with serenity. You need to read this!"

Rick Warren, pastor, founder of Saddleback Church, and bestselling author

"When we feel crushed by stress, most of us wish we could find practical counsel from a wise, trusted, proven friend who has lived through stress and knows how to thrive in it. This book enables us to get that kind of counsel from one of the most respected Christian leaders of our time. Some books seem to increase stress by promising quick fixes from people who have never been where we are. This book is different. It helps us in seasons of stress to see that we are not alone and equips us to find our way to the other side."

Russell Moore, public theologian, *Christianity Today*

"Vance Pitman is the master of applying biblical truths to the lives and routines of believers. This book, *The Stressless Life: Experiencing the Unshakable Presence of God's Indescribable Peace*, meets a huge need at a critical time. So many of us Christians need to grasp how Christ wants us to have the abundant life and not the stressful life. Indeed, this book is one of the most timely tomes I have read in years."

Thom S. Rainer, founder and CEO of Church Answers

"Books about escaping stress and finding peace may abound, but this book is one of a kind. As the book demonstrates, a stressless life comes not by mastering a few self-help techniques but by looking at God and the world in an entirely new way. By the time you get twenty—— your life the same."

J.D. Gree——rch

——\sk

D1114506

"I've seen Vance Pitman manage overwhelming stress with grace and wisdom. He lives the message of *The Stressless Life*, and I'm so thankful he has shared with us how we can live with less stress and more peace. This is a powerful book that can add remarkable value to your life."

Jud Wilhite, senior pastor of Central Church and author of *Uncaged*

"We live in a culture that tells us we need more. More money, more house, more platform, more beauty, more influence, more power. Along with our frenetic pace to get more, we also have acquired more stress. My friend Pastor Vance Pitman holds your hand through the pages of this book, teaching you how to have a stressless life. But be warned, this life of less stress will disrupt and sever your attachment to the 'more' so you can have more of Christ, his kingdom, and his peace."

Dr. Derwin L. Gray, lead pastor at Transformation Church and author of *God, Do You Hear Me?*

"Worry and anxiety are no respecters of persons. Keep living and these twins will try to break into our hearts and minds, robbing us of our peace. At no point has this been truer than in recent times. A global pandemic has pushed most of us into quarantine and onto the brink. Because of these realities, I can think of no better time than now and no better person to provide us with a providential resource on how we can experience the abundant life than my friend Pastor Vance Pitman."

Dr. Bryan Loritts, author of *The Dad Difference*

The
Stressless
Life

The Stressless Life

Experiencing the Unshakable
Presence of God's Indescribable Peace

VANCE PITMAN
WITH SAM O'NEAL

BakerBooks
a division of Baker Publishing Group
Grand Rapids, Michigan

© 2022 by Vance Pitman

Published by Baker Books
a division of Baker Publishing Group
PO Box 6287, Grand Rapids, MI 49516-6287
www.bakerbooks.com

Printed in the United States of America

Library of Congress Cataloging-in-Publication Data
Names: Pitman, Vance, author. | O'Neal, Sam, author.
Title: The stressless life : experiencing the unshakable presence of God's indescribable peace / Vance Pitman with Sam O'Neal.
Description: Grand Rapids, MI : Baker Books, a division of Baker Publishing Group [2022] |
Identifiers: LCCN 2021029294 | ISBN 9780801094620 (paperback) | ISBN 9781540902092 (casebound) | ISBN 9781493434091 (ebook)
Subjects: LCSH: Stress management—Religious aspects—Christianity.
Classification: LCC BV4509.5 .P568 2022 | DDC 248.4—dc23
LC record available at https://lccn.loc.gov/2021029294

Some names and identifying details have been changed to protect the privacy of individuals.

Published in association with Yates & Yates, www.yates2.com.

Baker Publishing Group publications use paper produced from sustainable forestry practices and post-consumer waste whenever possible.

22 23 24 25 26 27 28   7 6 5 4 3 2 1

To Travis and Darrell,
whose friendship and fellowship helped me put the pieces
back together and experience the unshakable
presence of God's indescribable peace.

Contents

9

Introduction

It was one of the strangest days of my life. I suppose it was one of the most frightening too, although I don't remember much of the scary stuff, given that I was basically unconscious. What I do remember was pretty routine: lots of work, lots of fires that needed to be put out, lots of meetings, and lots of pressure to get it all done as quickly as possible.

In other words, it was a pretty normal day—which, I guess, was a big part of the problem.

I'd been in the office for about ten hours when I decided to head home and spend some time with my family, but then planned to get back to work once everyone went to bed. I started to realize something was wrong at dinner. I didn't feel right. Didn't feel like myself. It seemed like I was moving in slow motion, both mentally and physically. I lost all motivation and energy, and I couldn't even bring myself to lift up my arm to bring food to my mouth. I had a hard time following the conversation between my wife and my kids.

I tried to push through it as usual, but by the end of the meal I was convinced something wasn't right. I dragged myself up to our bedroom and lay down. I fell asleep instantly. I didn't wake up for eight days.

When my family finally got me out of the house and dragged me to my doctor, I was diagnosed with the physical version of a mental breakdown. Basically, my body just quit. It shut down. Ran out of juice with no extra batteries in the drawer. Looking back on that period of my life, I'm surprised it didn't happen sooner.

We—myself; my wife, Kristie; and our launch team and ministry partners—founded Hope Church in Las Vegas, Nevada, back in 2001. From the very beginning, when eighteen people gathered in my living room, God's activity was overwhelmingly present. So were the challenges of ministry.

We outgrew our living room in four months. We reached the thousand-member threshold in four years, with hundreds of people coming to Christ each year during that period. Best of all, we'd planted a church in Sin City that itself would establish more churches in the West with a passion to engage the nations with the gospel—and that mission was progressing better than we'd dreamed. We had a network of churches joining together in God's global mission and growing rapidly.

All that was good news!

The bad news was that the demands and challenges of an intense ministry season had knocked me out of balance. I had taken on more than I was supposed to in my efforts to live out the calling Christ had placed on my life.

In short, my life was being squeezed by stress in almost every way imaginable, and I was failing the test. Hard.

Growing up as a pastor's kid in Alabama, I heard all the jokes about preachers being a little lazy. "It must be nice to work just one day a week," and on and on. So when I accepted God's call to the ministry, I wanted to show everyone that pastors work as hard as anyone else. Actually, I wanted to work harder than everyone else.

Of course, church planting is hard work, no matter where you do it. And church planting in a relatively unchurched area is harder still. But I was confident in my call, so I put my shoulder against the load and kept pressing forward. For about ten years I worked sixty or seventy hours a week, every week. That was my routine. My own expectation. I also did everything in my power to be a godly husband to my wife and a great dad to our four children. Again, all these priorities were correct, but the rhythm was wrong. I was functionally unaware of God's prescription for dealing with stress in a way that leads to peace.

From the outside looking in, everything was golden. But behind the curtain, we had just about every major problem a church could have. And I felt like all the solutions had to come through me.

Like many churches in the West, our biggest struggle was finding a place to meet. It's almost impossible for churches to get building loans in Las Vegas, so we held services in just about every location imaginable—from houses to schools to corporate conference centers to warehouses. The church met in nine different locations over the first ten years, but we were declined by over fifty lease properties during that same period. I even remember hopping in the car with some of our pastors one day and driving around the city looking for a place to hold our services *that coming week!*

Of course, God provided. But each time He moved to expand our fellowship, we'd outgrow our meeting space and be in danger of being homeless once again.

Most church plants struggle with finances, and we were no exception. We went for more than two years with literally no money in the bank—whatever we received through the offering each weekend went to paying whichever bills were most urgent. That's because Las Vegas was in a huge economic depression at the time, which also meant 30 percent of our congregation left the city because they couldn't find a job. We had moral failures and turmoil related to a couple of our staff members, including a pastor. We had to navigate the growing pains of an expanding, multigenerational congregation comprised of dozens of cultures, languages, and religious expectations. And on and on it went.

I didn't realize what was happening at the time, but in 2012, everything came to a head. That was the year we were scheduled to finish a multiyear building project so we could actually gather for worship and carry out ministry on our own campus. Unfortunately, that was also the year our bond company was sued and closed its doors, which meant we were short about 3.5 million dollars with three months to go before the building was finished—and no lending institution to help us pay the bills. I had to deal with sixty contractors threatening to walk off the job and sue the church. Daily.

Once the building was finally finished, we were on campus for only four and a half months when Las Vegas experienced a hundred-year flood. In a matter of hours, our entire campus—everything we'd poured ourselves into creating and preparing for the past few years—was under water. The flood happened so quickly that our staff were literally carried out of the building on the shoulders of fire and rescue personnel. Thankfully, nobody was seriously hurt, but the catastrophe caused over a million dollars in damages to our brand-new facility.

And wouldn't you know it; nobody has flood insurance in a desert.

So, yeah, that period of my life was a little crazy. We had a church with over 2,500 people gathering weekly, but I was still leading the same way as when we had eighteen people in my family's living room. I was in every meeting. Nobody knew the budget better than I did (or so I thought). Nobody could handle the preaching like I could (or so I believed). Whatever problems or situations needed answers, I felt I was the only one who could resolve them.

By the beginning of 2013, everything had caught up with me—the problems, the pressure, the tension, the anxiety. In other words, the stress.

I collapsed. For almost two hundred hours, I did nothing but sleep. I lost eighteen pounds because I couldn't even wake up long enough to eat. I couldn't talk with my wife, let alone my staff or congregation. My body simply refused to function.

We're All Stressed

Many people close to me will be surprised when they read about this incident from my past. I don't talk about it much. I don't even like thinking about it.

So why am I including it in this book? Because I want you to understand one important thing about me: I know what

15

it's like to be stressed. I know how it feels to be crushed by life's pressures and apprehensions.

I also understand I'm not the only one.

According to the American Institute of Stress, 77 percent of Americans regularly experience physical symptoms caused by stress.[1] That means stress is much more than simply feeling a heavy load or experiencing a busy schedule. It impacts your body in real and tangible ways, with symptoms that include headaches, loss of energy, chest pain, nausea, dizziness, and more. The same study says 48 percent of people lie awake at night and have difficulty sleeping because of stress.[2]

Let's stop here a moment, because I know many times numbers whoosh right over our heads without really sticking. Happens to me all the time. So let me illustrate what these numbers actually mean.

If you're at a meeting with ten people, there's a pretty good chance that eight of those people are physically impacted by the level of stress in their lives. Their bodies are affected. When you walk down the street, eight out of every ten people you pass are not as healthy as they should be because of the way stress and anxiety are affecting their ability to function.

The next time you go somewhere where a lot of people are gathered together—whether that's a church service or a big crowd at the grocery store, it doesn't matter—remind yourself that half of those people didn't get enough sleep the night before because of stress. Half! The next time you're stuck in traffic on the interstate, remember that half the people driving those cars didn't get enough sleep last night because of something that's stressing them out. Yikes! One out of every two.

Of course, things aren't getting any easier in terms of the world and the amount of stress it throws our way. I wrote this book during the final months of 2020—a year that at times felt like nothing but stress! This probably won't surprise you, but 67 percent of people said they experienced significantly more stress in 2020 than in previous years because of the COVID-19 pandemic.[3]

My point is this: we're all stressed. Doesn't matter if we're young or old, male or female, rich or poor, Republican or Democrat, hard-driving corporate executive or first-year intern, Christian or atheist—stress is a reality for everyone. Stress is a burden for everyone.

If you're fortunate enough to not be feeling that burden right now, I am so happy for you. I really am. But you need to understand that this stress-free period won't last. Sooner or later, you'll start to feel the pull against your shoulders. The tension. The drag. Sooner or later, the weight will start to pile up. And the more you try to fight it—the more you tell yourself to "suck it up" or experiment with different strategies to manage or medicate away the stress—the heavier that weight will become, until you eventually feel crushed by it. Totally beaten down.

That's the bad news.

The good news is that the *presence* of stress doesn't need to dominate your life. Yes, we all experience apprehension and anxiety—we can't escape from stress. But we can respond to stressful situations in a way that allows us to *enjoy* life, not just *endure* it.

> We can respond to stressful situations in a way that allows us to **enjoy** life, not just **endure** it.

In fact, we can live in a way that's

17

defined not by anxiety and apprehension but by the unshakable presence of God's indescribable peace.

I know that's possible because I've seen it happen in the lives of many people—including my own.

I'm not much of a tech wizard, so I was a little skeptical when my staff made me start using an iPhone several years ago. Everyone kept telling me about all the wonderful things it could do and all the ways it could save me time—but I wasn't sure. Nothing seemed to work for me as easily as everyone else described.

Then one of my daughters said, "Dad, if you have any trouble with the phone, just do a hard reset."

"A what?" I had no idea what she was talking about.

"Just hold down this button and this button at the same time," she said, "and keep holding them until an apple pops up on your screen. That will fix most of your problems."

Turns out she was right—and not just about the phone.

A hard reset is pretty much what happened to me after I took my unplanned, unwanted, and unforeseen weeklong nap. Once I was finally able to function for more than a few minutes at a time, my wife and some of the leaders of our church sat me down for an intervention of sorts. They told me my role and responsibilities at the church and in our other ministries would be cut back drastically. I was allowed to preach on the weekends but do nothing else. No meetings. No strategy sessions. No counseling. No conflict resolution. They also told me this new reality would last a long time—not days, not weeks, but months.

To their credit, they didn't give me a choice in any of these decisions. They told me what was going to happen during this reset period, and they made it clear that those closest to me would ruthlessly enforce my new way of life. I'm grateful to live and work with people who care about me enough to help me see how badly I was managing the stress in my life—and to help me choose a better path.

Just as importantly, I'm grateful that the months and years since that hard reset have allowed me to focus on the topic of stress and how it impacts our lives. I'm excited to share my journey with you and show you what I've learned as we move through the pages of this book.

What's the Alternative?

A lot of people have a lot of opinions about which holidays are best. I think most would put Christmas at the top of the list.

Not me, though. For my money, there's no better celebration than Thanksgiving.

I love everything about Thanksgiving Day. First and foremost, my house gets crammed full of the people I love most in the world—my children, my grandchildren, and my closest friends. Then there's the food. Kristie gets going on the preparations early in the morning, which means the smells start to tease and tantalize my nostrils just about as soon as I get up. By the time we finally sit down around the table, I'm usually drooling as much as the family dog. And, to top it all off, we get to watch football all day.

Seriously, what could be better on this side of heaven than Thanksgiving Day?

There comes a moment at every Thanksgiving feast when I finally throw in the towel. I've eaten seconds and thirds of everything on the table—even the veggies Kristie insists on serving to make the meal seem healthier. I've unbuckled my belt two plates ago, and now there is literally no more room in my stomach. I'm completely stuffed. Completely satisfied. So I push myself away from the table, lean my head back against the chair, wave my napkin like a white flag of surrender, and breathe out the most satisfied sigh you could imagine.

Do you know that feeling? Have you been there? Keep that image in mind while you read this passage from God's Word: "Abraham breathed his last and died at a good old age, an old man and satisfied with life; and he was gathered to his people" (Gen. 25:8).

If you're familiar with Abraham's story, you know he has a unique place in history as the forefather of both the Jewish and Arab people groups. He had a deep and personal connection with God that spanned decades. As a husband, father, and grandfather, he was dedicated to his family. And he lived as part businessman, part farmer, part soldier, and part priest.

In short, he enjoyed an incredible life. And when it finally came time for him to move on, he did so as someone satisfied with life. In other words, Abraham pushed back from life's table completely stuffed with blessings and fully satisfied by the wonder of everything he'd experienced.

As residents of the modern world, most of us understand that the stress we live and deal with every day is not good. It's not normal. It's life-taking rather than life-giving, which is why we're so desperate to find ways to manage or alleviate or otherwise eliminate anxiety from our lives.

What we often have a harder time understanding is the alternative. If stress is bad, what's the right way to live? What's life supposed to look like?

For me, the answer to that question is Abraham. He is the example not only of what life *could* be but also what it *should* be. That's because we weren't created by God to drag ourselves through each day in a haggard haze of stress. No! We were created to be so stuffed full of purpose and peace and the riches of God's blessings that we can't take even one more bite.

Or, as Jesus described it, we were created for abundant life: "The thief comes only to steal and kill and destroy; I came so that they would have life, and have *it abundantly*" (John 10:10, emphasis added).

What I'm saying is this: you and I were created for a stressless life. Not *less stress*. That's important. You and I were never intended to manage or deal with something as harmful and corrosive as stress. (More on that in chapter 1.) Instead, we've been given everything necessary to enjoy a life that is free from stress. Devoid of stress. A stressless life.

That's the unshakable promise you've been offered. That's the life I want you to live. And I'll show you how to find it in these pages.

Available Now

Too many of us believe Jesus's promise of abundant life was meant to be fulfilled in the distant future—either in heaven after we die or maybe here on earth after we pass some unseen milestone by earning enough money or developing enough patience or solving all the problems that weigh us down. (Hint: that unseen milestone doesn't exist and that future will never come.)

Thankfully, we don't have to wait to experience Jesus's promise of abundant life. We don't have to wait to figure out how to remove stress from each day. That life is available to us in the here and now. Today. Right this moment.

Let me say it again: that life is available to *you* in the here and now! Today! Right this moment! You don't have to wait until some later date to experience the stressless life. You don't have to become a sage or a psychiatry professor. You don't have to take a class or pay a price.

Instead, you can immediately take hold of the indescribable, soul-satisfying, joy-producing, fruit-bearing life God has always intended you to live. Of course, to do that, you'll need to learn what stress is and how to remove it from your life. And not just stress in a general sense, but the specific stressors pressing down on your neck even now. I'm talking about

- stress in your schedule,
- stress in your budget,
- stress in your relationships,
- stress in your decision-making,
- stress during spiritual battle,
- and stress caused by circumstances outside your control.

My goal in this book is to help you work through each of these issues and more. This isn't some magic bullet to make all your problems go away. That's not possible! Instead, these pages are filled with practical instruction and spiritual inspiration for moving away from anxiety and jumping feetfirst into the kind of abundant, stress-free living that is only available through Christ.

1

Anxious Living

What Is Stress and Why Is It Bad?

He didn't know it was the last football game he'd ever play, but Journey Brown made the most of it.

The 2019 Cotton Bowl featured the Penn State Nittany Lions against the Memphis Tigers. Brown was the starting running back for Penn State, and he played an incredible game: sixteen rushes for a total of 202 yards and two touchdowns. He ran around people. He ran through defenders. He was all over the field and seemingly unstoppable, leading his team to victory with a score of 53–39.

Going into the 2020 season, the future could not have been brighter for Journey Brown. Professional scouts from the National Football League (NFL) were already drooling over his explosiveness and breakaway speed. Coaches were talking about him. Sports reporters were writing articles about everything they expected him to achieve and all the awards they predicted he would win.

As a junior, Brown was poised not only for another successful season with Penn State but also to run all the way to the NFL in 2021, with a high position in the draft and a lucrative contract.

That's when everything changed.

In a tragic twist, a routine medical examination revealed that Brown suffered from hypertrophic cardiomyopathy, a condition that causes the muscle wall around the heart to become abnormally thick. As a result, the heart has to work much harder to pump blood—a dangerous reality for an elite athlete. In fact, hypertrophic cardiomyopathy is the most common cause of sudden cardiac death in people under thirty-five.

Journey Brown retired from football on November 11, 2020. "The pain of not being able to play the game I love anymore hurts, and I can't explain how I am feeling right now," he wrote in a letter to his teammates and fans. "However, I can walk away from the game knowing I truly gave my all at every practice, on every down, and in the locker room every day."[1]

One of the procedures used to diagnose hypertrophic cardiomyopathy is called a stress test. I've been through those myself. Doctors hook you up to a bunch of monitoring machines, then put you on a treadmill. They start you out slow but then increase the speed and inclination of the treadmill every three minutes. It doesn't take long to get most patients huffing and puffing!

Of course, that's the goal of a stress test. The whole process is designed to put extra pressure on your heart—to get it pushing and pumping beyond its normal capacity. That pressure, that stress, reveals anything out of the ordinary.

What Journey Brown discovered in November 2020 is that life itself is a stress test. I'm sure he hopped on that treadmill at his doctor's office believing it was all just another routine diagnostic. Just another run for an athlete who loved running. But then the results came back, and the entire trajectory of his life changed in a single moment. Dreams were crushed. The future was suddenly unclear.

Thankfully, he responded well. James Franklin, the head coach of Penn State's football team, called Brown's diagnosis "heartbreaking." But he also noted that Brown immediately began serving as a voluntary assistant coach for the other running backs on the team, and he believes the young man's future remains bright. "He's handled it better than I think anybody I've ever been around," said Franklin. "I don't know if he wants to stay in football or whatever he decides to do, but he's going to be unbelievably successful."[2]

Have you learned that life is a stress test? I want to focus on that principle for a moment because it lies at the very heart of this book.

Everything you experience in life is a stress test—successes, failures, relationships, work, family, sickness, uncertainty, finances, good times and dreams, bad times and tragedies—all of it increases the pressure on you and within you until your areas of weakness become clear. Sometimes that pressure increases gradually throughout your childhood and school and marriage and career. Or, as Brown experienced, sometimes that pressure gets piled up all at once in a moment of crisis.

What's the goal of all that pressure, you wonder? What's the point?

To reveal the condition of your heart.

What Is Stress, Anyway?

Before we go any further, let's make sure we're on the same page about this idea of stress (or anxiety or worry). Because the concept of stress generally (and those words individually) can mean different things to different people.

Here's how the dictionary defines *stress*:

- *Physiology.* A specific response by the body to a stimulus, as fear or pain, that disturbs or interferes with the normal physiological equilibrium of an organism.
- Physical, mental, or emotional strain or tension.[3]

Those definitions are technically accurate. They are semantically correct. But they don't really convey what it's like to experience stress in real life. Yes, stress is a physiological response within our bodies, but it's also much more than that. Yes, stress can be described as "strain" or "tension," but it's hard to articulate in any meaningful way what that actually feels like.

Below is a more true-to-life definition I came up with.

Stress: Fearful concern experienced when life's demands seem greater than my ability to meet them.

That definition fits better with my experiences with stress. I don't encounter stress every time I experience a challenge—

probably because I like challenges! I like digging in and doing the difficult work. But when I start to feel overwhelmed, when I start to feel like what's being demanded of me is more than my personal resources can cover, that's when I become stressed. This is the definition of stress we'll use throughout this book, so it's worth looking a little deeper to

> Stress is fearful concern experienced when life's demands seem greater than my ability to meet them.

unpack it. Specifically, I want to show you the difference between "stressors" and "stress," as well as the differences between "genuine concern" and "fearful concern."

Stressors vs. Stress

Stressors are those circumstances that create the levels of pressure, tension, and strain that lead to stress. They can be expected or unexpected. They can be big or small. They can be recurring incidents or a onetime event. Stressors are usually negative moments—things we didn't want to happen. But positive circumstances can also serve as stressors when they change our lives in big ways or when we're unprepared to receive them.

Most stressors we experience are relatively minor. Getting stuck in a traffic jam. Catching a cold. Receiving a bill or an invoice that is way more than we'd planned to spend. Falling into an argument with our spouse over something silly or unimportant. These are the kinds of inconveniences and annoyances each of us confronts on a daily basis.

Of course, minor doesn't mean easy. When our lives are filled with pressure and strain, even the smallest stressor can become the straw that breaks the camel's back.

Other stressors are so big they immediately take center stage in our lives. The loss of a job. Cancer. Divorce. The death of a parent or child. Stressors can also include larger events that may not impact us directly—wars, pandemics, political elections, economic depression, and so on. All these factors (and many more) can push us toward fearful concern.

In the introduction, I said that all people experience stress, and that's true. Yet it's important to understand that stress doesn't cause itself. Instead, what brings about stress are the various stressors we encounter in our lives. We could say it this way: *stressors* are what we face, while *stress* is what we feel. Stressors put demands on us that threaten to overwhelm our resources and can cause us to feel fear and worry and anxiety.

To say it another way, stressors are the primary sources of stress.

But we don't have to respond that way. It's possible to handle stressors in a way that produces peace. In fact, it's possible to enjoy a stressless life. Truly, it is! That's what this book is all about.

Before we move forward, I think it's necessary to point out that all people encounter all kinds of stressors every single day of their lives—including Christians. There's a lot of confusion about that reality, both in our culture and in the church. Many Jesus followers feel shame or guilt or doubt when they encounter trials and tough times. They feel like they must be doing something wrong or that God is punishing them.

The truth is, followers of Jesus are not immune to difficult circumstances. In fact, it's clear from Scripture that we should *expect* stressors in our lives.

The apostle Paul writes this to the church: "But realize this, that in the last days difficult times will come" (2 Tim. 3:1). The Amplified Bible defines the phrase *difficult times* as "times [of great stress and trouble] . . . [that will be hard to bear]." Have you experienced those times? I have. The apostle Peter adds this: "Beloved, do not be surprised at the fiery ordeal among you, which comes upon you for your testing, as though something strange were happening to you" (1 Pet. 4:12). Don't be surprised when you encounter a stressor! It's not something strange. It's not a confirmation that you're going down the wrong path. In fact, stressors and difficult circumstances are often signs that you're headed in the right direction spiritually; you're just encountering resistance from your enemy.

In short, what distinguishes us as followers of Jesus isn't the absence of stressors in our lives—it's not the absence of pressure or strain, or even danger or doubt. Instead, what distinguishes us is the unshakable presence of God's indescribable peace in the midst of these realities.

So here are the big questions you need to wrestle with for a minute: When you encounter difficult circumstances, do you experience stress or peace? When the pressures of life start to squeeze you, what comes out? Anxiety and worry and fear? Or is it, to use Paul's terminology from Philippians 4:7, "the peace of God, which surpasses all comprehension"? Indescribable peace.

Genuine Concern vs. Fearful Concern

My wife and I have four children, which means we're fluent in all the kids' movies. In fact, our family went through many different waves of kids' movies—and now, with grandchildren, we're smack in the middle of a whole new generation of kids' content.

The Lion King is one movie I remember, although that's mainly because of the music. Some of those songs are so catchy and repetitive that it felt almost impossible to shake them loose from my brain. We'd have kids singing them all over the house for weeks, and I'm man enough to admit that I joined in from time to time.

There is a song called "Hakuna Matata" that is especially memorable. It's sung by a young lion, a boar, and a meerkat walking through the jungle. I thought that was a strange combination, but the words have stuck with me. The song is about having no worries. It's about not letting anything bother you. It's about a problem-free philosophy you can carry around for the rest of your days.

Let me make this clear: "Hakuna Matata" is a great theme for a song, but it's a terrible philosophy for life.

That's because every person experiences what I call genuine concern. We all have things we care about—people, relationships, ideals, places, possessions, resources, memories, and more. We walk around with personal connections that carry weight and meaning, which means we have the potential to feel genuinely concerned when there's a problem associated with these people, ideals, or resources.

Such concern is natural. It's good. It's part of what it means to be human, and it's part of what it means to be created in the image of a loving God. The problem comes when our genuine concern drifts over a line and becomes fearful concern.

You're probably wondering, *What's the difference between genuine concern and fearful concern?* Good question. Fortunately, there's a simple answer.

30

- *Genuine concern* is expressed through a dependence on God. It causes us to ask, "What will He do?"
- *Fearful concern* is expressed through a dependence on self. It causes us to ask, "What am I going to do?"

The biblical term often connected to this idea of genuine concern is *burden*. When we encounter a stressor, or when a problem arises in connection with something or someone we care about, we feel the weight of that burden—often deeply. We feel genuinely concerned about the situation, and that's okay. Concern is not the issue.

The right response when we feel genuinely concerned is to carry that burden to God and lay it at His feet. The psalmist writes, "Cast your burden upon the LORD and He will sustain you" (Ps. 55:22). Peter says, "Therefore humble yourselves under the mighty hand of God, so that He may exalt you at the proper time, having cast all your anxiety on Him, because He cares about you" (1 Pet. 5:6–7).

On a practical level, that looks like this: *Lord, here is the situation. I don't have what it takes to fix this, but I know You do, so I'm placing this burden in Your hands.* And the result is peace.

On the flip side, fearful concern is when we refuse to let go of those burdens and instead keep piling them higher and higher on our shoulders. When we face a situation out of our hands or beyond our control *but try to handle it anyway*, we will inevitably feel stress. Anxiety. Worry.

And when our days are filled with fearful concerns of all shapes and sizes, we become so weighed down with questions, pressure, and stress that we begin to *endure* life rather than *enjoy* it.

31

Have you been there? Are you there now? If so, keep reading, because there is an answer. You can experience God's peace in every situation, and you can experience it right now. Today.

Why Should We Avoid Stress?

Have you ever wondered what the most venomous snake in the world is? The answer is the inland taipan, which lives in Australia. Taipans are big snakes—adults grow to between six and ten feet long—but they pack an even bigger punch within their fangs. Just one drop of venom is potent enough to kill one hundred adult men in as little as forty-five minutes.[4]

I've never lived in Australia, but imagine for a moment that you do. You have a nice house Down Under and a lovely property close to the ocean. The sun shines every day, you can smell the salt air from the sea, you love your local church, and you can still run to a local supermarket if you need groceries or other supplies.

The only problem is the taipans. They live all over your yard, which means anytime you leave the house, you're under threat from the world's most venomous creature. Talk about a stressor!

Imagine calling the Australian equivalent of an exterminator or animal control, but they just tell you that taipans are considered an endangered species—they can't be removed. Your only option is to deal with the situation as best as you can. "Just try to manage your interactions with the snakes," they say. "Don't go out any more than you need to, and do your best to keep a positive attitude whenever a snake is close by."

Wouldn't that be terrible advice? How insane would it be to live with such a dangerous threat or try to get by through limiting your exposure to such deadly creatures?

Yet that's exactly what we're taught to do with stress—manage it, live with it, carry as much anxiety and worry as we're able to bear, and then (and only then) look for help. In fact, a Google search on how to manage stress produces more than 1.2 billion results. No wonder so many people are failing the stress test of life. No wonder we lack peace. We've been told to manage something that is poisonous, and it's killing us one day at a time.

The real solution to the problem of stress in our lives is not to manage it but to eliminate it. Passing the stress test of life means ridding yourself of that stress; it means living a stressless life. In fact, let's conclude this chapter by exploring five reasons why you should be ruthless in removing stress from your life.

God Said So

There's no point in beating around the bush; the main reason we should avoid the presence of stress in our lives is because God told us to.

Jesus said, "For this reason I say to you, do not be worried about your life, as to what you will eat or what you will drink; nor for your body, as to what you will put on" (Matt. 6:25). Later, the apostle Paul repeated that idea more succinctly when he wrote, "Do not be anxious about anything" (Phil. 4:6).

In those verses, the words translated "worried" and "anxious" are both from the same root term in the Greek language. That's a term that means to care, to worry, to be troubled, or to be pulled in different directions. It's the idea of having something on your mind continuously that consumes you and weighs on you—you can't escape it.

Have you ever seen a dog "worrying" a bone? After they dig it up from whatever hiding place they used in the yard, they get it between their forepaws and then start chewing away. They gnaw on it and slobber all over it and just wear it down from one end to the other.

That's the picture described by this Greek word translated "worried" or "anxious." Stress is a fearful concern that keeps gnawing away at you. And God is clear in His Word that we should remove it from our lives.

Notice that both Jesus and Paul spoke in commands— "Do not be worried" and "Do not be anxious"—which means they weren't giving us options or suggestions. Which means removing stress from our lives is a requirement.

Once again, these commands aren't telling us to remove *every* stressor from our lives. That's impossible. Neither Jesus nor Paul is commanding us not to care about anything or to avoid all burdens and concerns. Instead, they are teaching that life's cares and concerns must be understood and processed through a right perspective of our relationship with God.

I like the way Albert Barnes talks about this:

Philippians 4:6 does not mean that we are to exercise no care about worldly matters—no care to preserve our property or to provide for our families; but that there is to be confidence in God as to free the mind from anxiety, and such a sense of dependence on Him as to keep it calm.[5]

Here's another way to think about it: allowing ourselves to become stressed and worried—and especially to saturate ourselves in a lifestyle of stress and worry—means we're stepping outside the boundaries God has set up for our lives. And those boundaries are for our protection. God didn't command us to avoid stress because it's lots of fun and He wants to hog it all for Himself. No! God commanded us to avoid stress because He knows it's not good for us and He wants us to experience what's best.

> Stress is displeasing to God. So when we willingly choose to tolerate fearful concern and anxiety, we are disobeying Him.

In short, stress is displeasing to God. So when we willingly choose to tolerate fearful concern and anxiety, we're disobeying Him.

Stress Is Actively Harmful

We also need to avoid stress because allowing it to become part of our lives is actively harmful. Stress endangers our health, physically, emotionally, and spiritually.

Physically, the statistics are staggering.

- 43 percent of adults suffer adverse health effects from stress.
- 75 to 90 percent of all visits to the doctor's office are for stress-related ailments and complaints.
- Stress costs American industries more than $300 billion every year through health-care expenses. (That's

more than the gross domestic product of over 160 nations!)[6]

- Stress is linked to the six leading causes of death in the modern world: heart disease, cancer, lung ailments, accidents, cirrhosis of the liver, and suicide.[7]

No wonder God said, "Don't do that!" Stress is harmful to our bodies. It hurts us.

Emotionally, stress has a wide range of harmful side effects. According to the Mayo Clinic, stress often causes restlessness and a lack of motivation or focus. It pushes people toward irritability and anger, and it also causes us to withdraw into sadness and depression. Anxiety and worry are major causes of overeating, anorexia, drug or alcohol abuse, addiction to nicotine, social withdrawal, and more.[8]

Spiritually, as we've already seen, living with stress puts us outside the boundaries of God's plan and purpose for our lives. Tolerating stress is an act of disobedience, which means it negatively impacts our relationship with God. It breaks our fellowship with Him and steals away the joy of the abundant life He's promised us.

My mentor, Clyde Cranford, says it this way: "Anxiety is a cancer that eats away at our flesh and our faith."[9]

God instructs us not to stress or worry or nurture anxiety because it is dangerous.

Stress Is Inconsistent with God's Character

I'm a big fan of A. W. Tozer, a pastor and author from Chicago during the early decades of the twentieth century. One of my favorite Tozer quotes is so simple yet so profound that it blows my mind each time I read it.

Here it is: "What comes into our minds when we think about God is the most important thing about us."[10] If you're like me, it takes a few seconds to process that principle because it's so deep. But let me walk you through a few ideas to show you not only what Tozer was saying but also why the presence of stress in our lives is inconsistent with God's character.

To start, how would you answer the following three questions?

- Is God loving?
- Is God wise?
- Is God powerful?

If you would answer yes to all three questions, you're mostly correct. That's because God is actually more than each of those attributes.

God is not only loving, but Scripture also says that "God *is* love" (1 John 4:8, emphasis added). God is not only wise, but all wisdom is contained in Him and flows from Him (see Col. 2:3). And God is not only powerful, but the Bible confirms in several places that He is all-powerful (see Isa. 40:26 and 2 Pet. 1:3, for example).

Based on these truths, we can make the following three statements:

- Since God is love, He desires only the best for us.
- Since God has all wisdom, He knows what is best for us.
- Since God is all-powerful, He can bring about what is best for us.

Now, here's the kicker: if all that is true, what are we so stressed about?!

Tozer understood that a wrong view of God (or even a "lesser" view) will have repercussions in our lives. That's because the more we misunderstand God and His character, the more we will rely on ourselves and our own resources— which causes stress. It produces that fearful concern.

For that reason, stress and anxiety and worry are inconsistent with the character of God, who desires what is best, knows what is best, and is always able to bring about what is best.

Stress Misrepresents God's Character to Others

Not only is the presence of stress in our lives inconsistent with God's character, but it paints a flawed picture of God for the rest of the world to see. Because our lives aren't just about you and me.

It was Thanksgiving morning when my friend Matt Chandler brewed himself a cup of coffee, then sat on his couch to feed his six-month-old daughter. The last thing he remembers from that day is putting his little girl in her bouncy seat. In the next moment, Matt collapsed near the fireplace, suffering a seizure so intense that he bit through his own tongue.

The next days and weeks were a whirlwind of crazy. Matt was diagnosed with a tumor on the frontal lobe of his brain. Emergency surgery was scheduled and carried out. Afterward, doctors informed Matt and his wife, Lauren, that the tumor was malignant. Worse, they were unable to remove all of it. And worse still, the cancer had likely spread to other areas of his brain.

That was back in 2009. I remember hearing about Matt's story from mutual friends. It captured my attention for two reasons. First, like me, Matt was a young pastor of a fast-growing church. I understood the pressures he must have been facing, and I couldn't imagine what it would be like to endure that pressure in the midst of such an immediate personal tragedy.

The second reason Matt's story caught my attention was because of the incredible peace he possessed. Despite the bad news and the physical strain, Matt sought to comfort those who cared about him, including his young congregation. He posted messages emphasizing God's character and sovereignty. He was visibly calm and collected whenever he preached a sermon or gave an interview. And as the story caught fire, he used whatever spotlight came his way to point people to the truth of the gospel.

Here's an example of what I mean from an interview Matt gave a year after his diagnosis:

> I believe the Scriptures teach that God is aware of every act at every level of the universe. From a star exploding to the rate at which our planet spins to a cell dividing, He knows. I don't believe in the end that God gave me cancer, but He certainly could have stopped it and didn't. So I have to believe—like Joseph, John the Baptist, and Paul had to believe when they were in prison—that God is working, and what the enemy means for evil, He will turn to good.[11]

Talk about unshakable peace! Matt Chandler passed the stress test. He showed a watching world what it truly means to believe that God loves us, God knows what is best, and God is able to bring about what is best.

Unfortunately, many followers of Jesus don't always react so well to the stress test of life—myself included. When we carry worry and anxiety, we present a distorted view of God to those who are watching our lives. And believe me, if you have made it known that you're a follower of Jesus, people are watching!

The reality is that stress in our lives misrepresents God's character to others. It raises questions about Him. *Is God really in control? Does He really care? Can we trust Him?*

Therefore, it needs to go. And in its place, we must both develop and display God's indescribable peace.

Stress Changes Nothing

The final reason we should get rid of the stress in our lives is because stress is pointless. It accomplishes nothing and changes nothing—at least, nothing good. As we've seen, stress can change plenty of things in terms of the negative impact it has on us, but it doesn't produce anything for our benefit.

That's what Jesus tells us in the Gospel of Luke. He was teaching His disciples when He said, "And which of you by worrying can add a day to his life's span? Therefore if you cannot do even a very little thing, why do you worry about the other things?" (Luke 12:25–26). The NIV translates verse 25 this way: "Who of you by worrying can add a single hour to your life?"

I'm guessing that doesn't surprise you. I know I've never had an epiphany or some kind of spontaneous blessing in my life because I was so stressed out. I've certainly never added anything good to my life because of worry or anxiety or doubt—it's been only subtraction. I'll bet the same is true for you.

Look one more time at our definition of stress: *Fearful concern experienced when life's demands seem greater than my ability to meet them.* I know you've been there. I know you've felt the crushing and the squeezing that always come with fearful concern— with stress. Me too. The good news is you don't have to carry it anymore. You don't have to be crushed anymore. You don't have to feel squeezed anymore. Yes, stressors will always be in your life—there will be people, problems, and circumstances that are difficult or troubling or way too much to handle.

But stressors don't have to lead to stress. You can pass the stress test of life, and as we'll see in the next chapter, it starts by understanding the incredible, indescribable, unshakable peace that has been offered to you by Jesus Christ.

2

Abundant Life

What Is God's Peace
and How Do I Find It?

It was December 20, 2014—less than a week until Christmas—
when Rolanda Collins received the worst news a mother and
grandmother could ever receive: her daughter, Martia, and
two young grandsons, Tyrone and Tobias, had been killed.
They were murdered along with Martia's boyfriend, De-
montae Rhodes.

The next weeks and months were a whirlwind of pain
for Collins and her family, even as the local justice system
ground into action. Police identified a suspect for the shoot-
ings: Calvin Carter, Martia's ex-boyfriend. The evidence
was clear that he broke into Martia's apartment and killed
everyone he found there, including the children.

During the trial, Collins had harsh words for Carter from the witness stand, expressing her desire that he be locked up for life. "May the same demons you worshipped terrorize your soul in hell," she added.[1]

Ultimately, Calvin Carter was tried, convicted, and sentenced to four life terms, plus 280 years in prison.

Collins hoped to address her family's tormenter once more during the official sentencing, but Carter waived his right to attend the hearing. "I was thinking it was going to give me a release," Collins said. She wanted to show this young man how his actions had affected her family. "I wanted him to feel the pain."[2]

In the years after the trial, Rolanda Collins did everything she could to regain some sense of normalcy in her life. She worked. She went to church. She visited with friends and neighbors. She endured the grieving process. She even set up a nonprofit ministry, called A Mother's Prayer, in her daughter's memory, with the goal of neutralizing violence and restoring hope in her community.

None of it worked. None of it helped her move past the ache of her loss, and none of it made life seem tolerable again—let alone joyful. In other words, none of it brought Mrs. Collins what she was desperate to find: peace.

I hope you never go through a tragedy like Rolanda Collins experienced. The pain she endured is something most people wouldn't be able to imagine. Yet no matter what your future holds, you will find yourself searching for the same thing she did—peace. I know that because all of us are searching for peace. Each of us is looking for peace with ourselves, peace with the world, peace with God, and peace with our purpose in life.

Remember what I mentioned in the previous chapter about 1.2 billion search results for "how to manage stress"? Stress is a destructive force in our lives, but the absence of stress isn't all we're seeking and striving for. No, we as human beings are desperate to experience something good. Namely, we're born with a longing for the inner sense of rightness and goodness that's summed up in the word *peace*.

Thankfully, we can find peace. We can not only find it but also be filled with it. And we can be filled, not only with a generic, general kind of peace, but with God's peace—what Scripture describes as "the peace of God, which surpasses all comprehension" (Phil. 4:7).

Rolanda Collins found that peace. After moving to Wisconsin, she began attending a new church—one that specialized in the ministry of healing, both physically and emotionally. That's where she felt convicted that God wanted her to forgive the man who killed her daughter and grandsons. In her words, "I needed to forgive my daughter's murderer in order to become free."[3]

Incredibly, that's exactly what she did. "I decreed and declared, 'I forgive you, Calvin Carter, for what you took from me, for what you did to my daughter and my grandchildren.' I said it and I said it from my heart. My life has not been the same since."[4]

What an amazing act of forgiveness! Mrs. Collins is a new hero of mine, and she received a hero's reward. "I have found so much peace," she said, "and I've developed a deeper level with Christ."[5]

Let me remind you that passing the stress test we call life doesn't mean removing any and all stressors from your day-to-day experiences; it's not about the absence of difficulties.

Instead, it's about the presence of God's peace in the midst of those difficulties. That's what abundant life is all about, and that's how to experience a stressless life.

If you're ready for that kind of life—for that kind of peace—keep reading. Because you can discover it today.

You Have Two Options

Let's go back to the key Scripture passage we've been focusing on so far in these pages. Writing to the church in Philippi, the apostle Paul gave these commands to all Christians, including you and me: "Do not be anxious about anything, but in everything by prayer and pleading with thanksgiving let your requests be made known to God" (Phil. 4:6).

Concentrate for a moment on the word *but*. In the original Greek language, that term is a participle of contrast. It's a stopping point designed to get the reader's attention—something that communicates antithesis or opposition.

What Paul is basically saying is that we have two options whenever we face difficulties in our lives. He points to the first option in the first part of the verse: we can get anxious. That's our natural response when our circumstances are demanding more from us than we have to offer, and it causes stress. We saw in the last chapter how damaging stress can be, which is why Paul says to avoid it. "Do not be anxious about anything" (Phil. 4:6).

The second option comes in the second part of the verse. Paul gives an alternative—to show the antithesis of stressing out. Let's read it again: "But in everything by prayer and pleading with thanksgiving let your requests be made known to God."

Abundant Life

That's the option we'll focus on in this chapter. Specifically, we're going to walk through four steps we can take to experience God's peace. But first, let's make sure we're on the same page about the concept of peace itself. Namely, what is peace and why should we want it?

What Is Peace?

Do you remember our definition for *stress* from the previous chapter? Stress is *fearful concern experienced when life's demands seem greater than my ability to meet them.* It's that pressure or panic or squeezing that we experience when we become aware that we can't handle a situation—and we try to handle it anyway.

What about *peace*, then? I define it this way:

> ***Peace:*** *The sense of divine favor arising from confidence in God and your relationship with Him.*

Peace is a sense of divine favor, and the key word there is *divine*. Because remember, we're talking about God's peace. We're not talking about the generic peace that comes from a simple absence of conflict. Anyone can experience that. Anyone can feel peaceful when everything is going well and there are no difficulties to struggle through.

No, we're talking about a peace that comes from God—a peace that has its source in God and is sown or grown in us through the abiding presence of the Holy Spirit. A peace that is both unshakable and indescribable.

> Peace is the sense of divine favor arising from confidence in God and your relationship with Him.

Have you seen that kind of peace in action? Have you witnessed people who are going through terrible circumstances, yet they seem unfazed? They even seem hopeful. Or, crazier still, they seem grateful.

Haven't you wondered how that could be? *How can they be so peaceful when everything around them is collapsing? How can they stay calm, or how can they keep their head held high when so much has gone wrong? How can Rolanda Collins offer forgiveness, and actually deepen her relationship with Christ, after her daughter and grandsons were murdered?*

The answer is, they can't. Not on their own. They're exhibiting God's peace. They've been filled with the peace that surpasses all comprehension.

Look back at the second part of our definition for peace: it's the sense of divine favor arising from confidence in God and your relationship with Him. We don't receive God's peace because we believe in ourselves or have a good support system. We receive God's peace when we believe the truth of Scripture that God loves us, knows what's best for us, and is able to bring about what's best in our lives.

That's critical because it points to the necessity of faith in our pursuit of abundant life.

Earlier I pointed to Abraham as our picture for abundant life. Abraham was a man of great faith. Scripture says he "believed God, and it was credited to him as righteousness" (Rom. 4:3). No matter what Abraham went through—and he endured a lot of trouble in his life, some of it caused by others and some caused by his own poor decisions—Abraham remained confident in God. He believed God was faithful.

That's why Scripture says that, at the end of his days, "Abraham breathed his last and died at a good old age, an old man and satisfied with life; and he was gathered to his people" (Gen. 25:8).

Abraham left this life completely satisfied with God's blessings, not because of his own ability or his own mental toughness. No, he was confident in God and confident in his relationship with God. Therefore, Abraham was filled with peace.

Why Should We Want Peace?

Now that we have a better understanding of what peace is, let's briefly consider why we should strive after it. What does it actually bring to our lives?

Well, as we've just seen, peace is a necessary ingredient for the abundant life Jesus promised in John 10:10. "The thief comes only to steal and kill and destroy," He warned. That "thief" is Satan. Our enemy. And Satan wants nothing more than for our lives to be so squeezed and so crushed down because of stress that we simply try to make it through each day. Satan wants to steal our joy, kill our hope, and destroy our sense of purpose until we simply endure life the way a lab rat endures a maze.

That's not what God wants for us, though. Jesus said, "I came so that they would have life, and have it abundantly" (John 10:10).

The only way that can happen is through God's peace. The only way we can truly enjoy the abundance of the life God planned for us is when we're filled with His peace that surpasses all comprehension—because that peace will carry us through our hardest seasons.

There's another reason we should want God's peace, and we can find it by looking back at Paul's instructions in

Philippians 4. We've already seen the commands Paul gave in verse 6: *Do not be anxious about anything* and *let your requests be made known to God.* The next verse includes a promise: "And the peace of God, which surpasses all comprehension, will guard your hearts and minds in Christ Jesus" (v. 7).

So not only does God's peace relieve us of stress during stressful situations we encounter in the present, but it also guards our hearts and minds against stress in the future.

Here's a picture of how that works. If you have a computer, some form of antivirus software is running on that device. You typically don't see it operating, but the software keeps an eye on everything that happens when you visit websites, check your email, play a game, watch a movie, and so on. What's interesting is that the software has multiple ways of protecting your computer. First, it actively scans all the files and programs trying to access your computer to make sure nothing bad is happening. The software also keeps a database of the threats it encounters not only on your computer but also on every computer around the world using that same software. The longer your antivirus software is in action and the more it becomes familiar with the different threats out there in cyberspace, the better it's able to protect your computer from both current and future problems.

In the same way, God's peace helps you build a wall of protection around your heart and mind against stress's destructiveness. That happens first when you encounter stressors. When life squeezes you with a burden and you hand it over to God, you'll find peace. But that also happens during the regular moments of your life. The more you grow in your relationship with God, and the more confident you become in His goodness and His character, the better your heart and mind will be protected, supported, and stabilized when stressors come back around again.

Now, having said all that, here are the big questions: Do you have God's peace? Have you been filled with the peace that surpasses all comprehension?

If not, let me show you how.

Know God

The first step to being filled with God's peace is to have a genuine relationship with God. To know God. In fact, here's a principle that serves as a foundation for this entire chapter: *you cannot know the peace of God without knowing the God of peace.*

Now, that's a problem because of the reality of sin. If you don't like that word, I understand. I don't like it either. I also don't like the word *taxes*, but that doesn't mean I can ignore taxes and assume they don't apply to my life. The same is true for sin.

> You cannot know the peace of God without knowing the God of peace.

The Bible says all people were created to enjoy fellowship with God. We were created to live in a relationship with Him, just as we were created to breathe air and consume food. Tragically, the presence of sin in our lives disrupts that relationship. In fact, the Bible teaches that since Adam and Eve sinned in the garden of Eden, every single human being who's been born into this world has been born dead to God, alive to sin, and without a relationship with God.

51

Thankfully, that's not all the Bible teaches. Scripture also says God loves us way too much to leave us in that condition. The message of the gospel—what we in the church call the "good news"—is that God took on human flesh and came to earth in the person of Jesus. God came to us to solve the problem of sin. Specifically, Jesus lived a sinless life as both God and man, and then Jesus offered Himself as a sacrifice on the cross to pay the penalty of our sin against God.

Jesus didn't stay dead, though! The reason the good news is good news is because Jesus rose from the grave as a testimony that God had accepted His sacrifice for our sin and that Jesus Himself had conquered death. What that means for humanity is that we can now turn away from our sin, put our faith in Jesus Christ, and be born again—this time born dead to sin, alive to God, and fully connected in a relationship with Him.

That's the revolutionary message of the gospel—the good news of Jesus Christ. And that's the very first step to being filled with God's peace. We can't experience God's peace until we experience God Himself. And the reality is, you can embrace this good news and take the first step to knowing God's peace right now. If you've never come to know God, right in this moment you can take a step of faith and believe in Him and experience His peace.

Paul knew this, which is why he writes the following in Philippians 4: "Not that I speak from need, for I have learned to be content in whatever circumstances I am. I know how to get along with little, and I also know how to live in prosperity; in any and every circumstance I have learned the secret of being filled and going hungry, both of having abundance and suffering need" (vv. 11–12).

What a wonderful description of God's peace. Paul said he could feel content in any situation. Why? Because he had learned the secret of experiencing God's peace.

What was that secret? Look at verse 13: "I can do all things through Him who strengthens me." The secret was the presence of Jesus in his life. The secret, or the foundation, of Paul's peace was his love relationship with God.

Remember the principle: You cannot know the peace of God until you know the God of peace. If you don't know the God of peace, before reading any further, cry out to Him right now in faith.

Live in Constant Fellowship with God

The first step to being filled with God's peace is to know God—to have a genuine, living relationship with Him. The second step is to actively and intentionally live each moment of your life in fellowship with God through that relationship.

Now, we talk a lot about fellowship at Hope Church in Las Vegas. It's part of our DNA. But when we talk about fellowship, we don't mean just our relationship with other believers—fellowship meals, potlucks, small groups, weeknight gatherings, Sunday morning services, and all that. Yes, those are important within the life of a church. And yes, building relationships with other believers is a necessary part of our spiritual lives. But our ability to enjoy fellowship with other believers is rooted and grounded in our fellowship with Jesus.

As a pastor, I find my passion is to point people toward a daily, intimate fellowship relationship with Jesus. My main goal personally, as a Jesus follower, is to know Jesus. To talk with Him and hear His voice. To seek His face. To live my life in a genuine, two-way, real-life relationship with my Savior. And I want the same for all Jesus followers.

That's what Paul is showing us in the second half of Philippians 4:6: "In everything by prayer and pleading with thanksgiving let your requests be made known to God." He's urging us to experience God's peace by living our lives in constant fellowship with Him.

A lot of specific words in that verse point to the same idea—*prayer*, *pleading*, *requests*, *made known*. These are terms that describe our communication with God. Talking with God.

Each term hinges on that critical phrase: "in everything." And let me be clear here. "Everything" means everything. Paul isn't saying to talk with God only about the important stuff. He isn't saying we should pray or plead or make ourselves known only when something comes along that we don't think we can handle. No, he says to talk with God "in everything."

Living in fellowship with God means being aware of His presence in every moment of our lives. And not just being aware of His presence but resting and abiding in His closeness and care. It means inviting God into every part of our day not just by "believing" He is there but by communicating with Him. Fellowshipping with Him.

The problem is most of us treat God like an app.

I'm a big fan of college football, so I have the ESPN app on my phone. That way, whenever I'm curious about the latest news or if I want to see the scores from last night's games, I can pull out my phone, view the app, get the information I need, and then put everything away again. I do the same thing with my weather app—although that's usually when I'm traveling, because the weather just doesn't change that much in my hometown of Las Vegas.

Now, I'm not knocking apps. I love how convenient they are. We open the app, we get what we need, we close the app, and then we move on with our day.

The problem is many of us Jesus followers have a "God app" in our minds. We open the app on Sunday mornings so we can spend some time worshiping and learning from God's Word, then we close it to have a nice lunch or watch some football. We open the God app during our "devotional time" in the mornings, then we close it once we're ready to start the rest of our day. And of course, we open the God app when something bad happens so that we can pray and ask God to help.

Do you see the problem? That's not how fellowship works. That's not how relationship works. God is not an app we can open and close, and He's not a box we can keep on a shelf until we need something from Him. God is a Person, and the only way to know that Person and experience His peace is through a genuine relationship.

Right about now you might be thinking, *Vance, I've heard all this before. I know I'm supposed to pray. I know I'm supposed to spend time with God. I know I'm supposed to grow in my relationship with Him.*

That's great. Knowing things is important. But let me ask you the million-dollar question. Are you putting your knowledge into practice? Are you living out these realities each day? Do you communicate with God "in everything," or is He an app you access every now and again? Are you living your life in constant fellowship with Him?

I don't ask these questions to be sarcastic or out of a sense of superiority. I'm a pastor's kid who became a pastor. I grew up in the church, and for a lot of years, I thought I knew everything about what it means to follow God. But then life hit. I began to get squeezed by the reality that life's demands are way more than I can handle using my own resources. And I realized that all these things I read in Scripture and learned in church aren't just helpful tips for being a spiritual person—they are necessary for me to experience the kind of life I want to experience. A life of abundance and purpose. A life of peace.

To say that more succinctly, everything in my life rises and falls on my personal fellowship with Jesus.

Here's what it looks like to live in constant fellowship with God. During the regular moments of your day—the nonstressful times—it means keeping a running conversation with God.

- "Lord, thank You for that breakfast. That was delicious."
- "Jesus, I'm feeling frustrated and impatient because of this traffic jam right now, and I know those emotions don't come from You. I say no to these feelings. I don't accept them. Please fill me with patience."
- "Father, this is the third time I've had to correct my daughter in the past hour. Please give me wisdom. Please help me train her in the way she should go."
- "Holy Spirit, please direct my thoughts during this meeting. I want to make a good impression, and I want to represent You well."

Living in constant fellowship means inviting God into every moment of your life. And the best way to be active and intentional about doing that is simply to talk with Him—and listen to Him—as you go about your day. Now, the stressors will still come, and some circumstances will be challenging. Even terrifying. You will face things that seem impossible to handle. Normally, in those moments, we turn our thoughts inward: *What am I going to do about this? How am I going to handle this? How can I get out of this? How in the world can I overcome this?* And before we know it, we're stressed.

> Everything in my life rises and falls on my personal fellowship with Jesus.

In my own life, living in fellowship with God means instead of looking within to my own abilities and resources—instead of frantically trying to figure things out on my own—I talk to God. I continue that conversation and tell Him what's going on. I tell Him what I'm feeling. And I ask Him to please show me how He plans to resolve the situation.

It's not magic, and talking to God won't necessarily solve the situation. But it will fill you with His peace.

Be Completely Honest with God

The third key to experiencing God's peace is to be completely honest with Him about your cares and concerns.

Paul writes, "In everything by prayer and pleading with thanksgiving let your requests be made known to God" (Phil. 4:6). That word *pleading* means to make your needs known. It's often translated as "supplication" or "petition."

If you've noticed a sense of desperation in those terms, you're correct. Being filled with God's peace comes when we completely open our hearts to Him. It means we expose ourselves to Him in a way that is vulnerable—even to the point of revealing our weaknesses and those parts of us that make us ashamed.

Here's what that might look like: *God, You can see what's going on here, and You know I don't have the resources to handle this. I don't have the strength to fix this. And to be honest, I'm starting to get stressed out, which I know I'm not supposed to do. So I am going to lay this situation at Your feet.*

Being honest with God is part of living in fellowship with Him. It's also important to be specific. For example, it's one thing to pray, *Lord, please help me with my financial needs.* It's quite another thing (and way more honest) to pray, *Lord, I just got a medical bill for $1,428.07, and I only have $887.88 in my checking account. You're in charge of all the resources in the universe, and I trust You're going to provide the $500 I need and more.*

In many ways, being honest with God sounds easy. He already knows everything, right? Even so, most of us aren't honest with Him. We try to hide ourselves—or certain parts of our thoughts, actions, or desires—from Him.

Why do we hide? Because of fear.

Remember all the way back to the garden of Eden? What did Adam and Eve do after they sinned by disobeying God's command? "Now they heard the sound of the LORD God walking in the garden in the cool of the day, and the man and his wife hid themselves from the presence of the LORD God among the trees of the garden" (Gen. 3:8). When God called out to His children, Adam said, "I heard the sound of You in the garden, and I was afraid because I was naked; so I hid myself" (v. 10).

Throughout all of human history since the fall, we've been hiding from God because we're afraid to be honest with Him. To be vulnerable. To allow Him to see the parts of us that are corrupted and stained by our sin.

What has all that hiding gotten us? More stress! Hiding from God is stressful, and it prevents us from being filled with His peace.

Here's a quick illustration of this idea. All my children are gifted by God in their own way. One of them, however, struggled with math growing up. This child didn't like math, resisted every attempt to get better at it, and just wasn't naturally gifted as a mathematician. Imagine our surprise, then, when that child scored a perfect 100 percent on a big math test one day. At that time, Kristie was homeschooling using an online curriculum, and she pulled me aside to show me the score.

Naturally, we were a little skeptical about this miracle grade. So we talked to this particular child to ask how they had done so well. Their response was: "It just came to me."

Yep, that sounded pretty fishy. We asked the child to show their work, and after just a little investigation, it became clear that our child had cheated on the test—which led to an important conversation about honesty and integrity.

Now, do you think that situation changed the level of love I felt toward my child? No! Do you think I lose love for any of my children when they disobey me or take a wrong step? Of course not. To this day, there's nothing they could do that would make me love them even a sliver less than I do right now. Not even close.

We often forget that God loves us with an even greater love than we have for our children. When we approach God in prayer, we're beloved children talking to our Father. It's so easy to believe we have to earn God's love. It's so easy to feel that if God saw who we really are—if He knew what goes through our minds or what we're capable of—He would love us less or reject us altogether. It's so easy to think we have to clean ourselves up and fix those shameful areas before we can approach our Father.

None of those statements are true. Why? Because our position with God isn't rooted in our performance for Him. Instead, our position with God is rooted in the person of Jesus Christ and His finished work on the cross. When we say yes to God's gift of salvation and become a Jesus follower, nothing in heaven or on earth can disconnect us from God or change the depth of His love for us.

That's why Paul said, "Cast all your anxiety on [God], because He cares about you" (1 Pet. 5:7). The word *cares* was written in the present-active tense in the original Greek language, which means it's ongoing. It doesn't stop. We could literally translate that verse "cast all your anxiety on God, because He continuously cares about you."

Be Intentional about Thanking God

To be filled with God's peace, we must know God, we must live our lives in constant fellowship with Him, we must be completely honest with Him, and we must be intentional about giving thanks to God in the different situations of our lives—but especially during stressful times.

Before we talk about thankfulness, let me mention that

these four steps to experiencing God's peace are interdependent, meaning they're connected. I'm not saying we should make fellowship with God a priority on Mondays and Fridays, honesty a priority on Thursdays, and then be thankful whenever we can. No. If we want to be saturated in God's peace, we need to build our daily lives and rhythms around all four principles. Look again at Philippians 4:6: "Do not be anxious about anything, but in everything by prayer and pleading with thanksgiving let your requests be made known to God."

This concept of thanksgiving is another thing we already know we're supposed to have. It's been drilled into our heads by our culture, by our parents, by the church. *Be thankful. Be thankful. Be thankful.* You already know this principle.

But let me ask you this: Are you putting your knowledge into practice? Are you thankful? Are you intentional about expressing your gratitude to God on a regular basis? Choosing to be thankful is generally a good policy for life, but it's especially valuable during difficult times. So let me repeat what I wrote a few paragraphs ago: we must be intentional about giving thanks to God in the different situations of our lives—but especially during stressful times.

Right now, you're probably thinking, *Huh? You've been telling me for two chapters that stress is harmful. So why would I thank God during stressful situations? Thank Him for what?*

Here's the principle I want you to understand: every struggle you encounter in life is an opportunity for God to demonstrate His faithfulness. Therefore, every difficulty you face is an opportunity to express thanks to God for the ways He is about to move.

Here's what that looks like: *God, You see what's going on here. You know what this is doing to me inside, and You know I don't have the resources to deal with this—but I trust You do. So here is the need I am facing, and I'm intentionally laying this burden at Your feet. Lord Jesus, thank You for what You're about to do. Thank You for giving me the chance to see Your faithfulness in action.*

Maybe right now you're thinking, *That's nice, but I don't feel thankful.* That's a great point. But the reality is, you don't have to feel an emotion in order to make a decision or a declaration. You don't have to *feel* thankful in order to *be* thankful.

In fact, I love what my mentor, Clyde Cranford, writes about this subject: "Feelings follow faith. Thus thankfulness is the result of thanksgiving. And worry and genuine thankfulness cannot abide in the same heart."[6]

Feelings follow faith. When you're intentional about expressing gratitude to God each and every day, the feelings will come. More importantly, you'll have a much greater awareness of all the ways God blesses you and all the reasons you have to be thankful, which will only increase your fellowship with God and give you more confidence to be open and honest with Him.

If you're feeling skeptical right now, I understand. I really do. Maybe four steps to being filled with peace sound just a little too easy, or maybe you've already heard all this before.

Here's my request: try it. In fact, this is more than a request. As someone who cares for you and wants you to experience the abundant life Jesus promised you, I'm begging and pleading with you to try it. If you have a relationship with God, make an active effort this week to live in constant fellowship with God. Be completely open and honest with Him. And be intentional about expressing gratitude to Him. If I'm wrong, I'll apologize, and you'll lose nothing. But I know from my individual experiences, my experiences as a pastor, and the promises of Scripture that I'm right—which means you can be filled with the unshakable, indescribable peace of God. You can live a stressless life. And it can happen right now. Today.

3

Running Out of Time

How Do I Find God's Peace in My Schedule?

Human beings, both as individuals and collectively, are capable of incredible things. Human beings can also be a bit strange at times—a little weird. And some human beings have a lot of time on their hands.

If you want to see the intersection between those three statements, check out the *Guinness World Records*.

First published in August 1955, the *Guinness World Records* was an instant hit and quickly became an icon of Western culture. Generations of people have flipped through the pages of each year's edition to read about the craziest accomplishments imaginable—not to mention those that are silly, strange, scary, and seriously impressive.

In recent years, the Guinness World Records brand has flourished again because of the internet and social media. Now people don't have to be content with reading about new world records; they can actually watch them be achieved online.

I came across one of those new records recently that really blew my mind. It was a video of a teenager from China named Que Jianyu. When I started watching the video, it looked like Que was juggling three Rubik's Cubes—those multicolored toys you twist and turn until each side of the cube is the same color. I thought that was pretty impressive. I can't juggle at all, and here this young man was making it look easy.

Then the video went into slow motion, and I saw what was actually happening. Que Jianyu wasn't just juggling those cubes—he was actually solving each of the puzzles *as he juggled them*! He'd catch one of the cubes in one hand, make a twist using just a couple of fingers, toss the cube back into the air, catch another one, make another twist, toss that one up again, catch the third, twist, and so on. I couldn't believe what I was seeing! Here's the craziest part: he solved all three Rubik's Cubes in just five minutes. I also thought the title of the record was pretty funny. Que Jianyu is the world record holder for "The Fastest Time to Solve Three Rubik's Cubes Whilst Juggling."[1]

You know what I've realized in recent years? All people are jugglers. We may not all be as good as Que Jianyu, but we're all juggling. Don't believe me? Think back to everything you've experienced this week. On a daily basis, you've been juggling your job, your kids, your favorite TV shows, your desire to be healthy, your desire for tasty food, your spouse, your commute, your daily quiet time, your need for sleep, your alarm clock, your household chores, your favorite hobbies, your small group, your phone calls, your social media accounts, your regular church service, your personal hygiene, and probably a whole lot more.

On a more general level, each of us is walking through this journey we call life while juggling a load of priorities that all feel incredibly important. I'm talking about marriage, parenting, relationships, finances, spirituality, physical health, emotional health, dreams and goals, fears and failures—not to mention our relationship with God.

Does that sound like a lot? That's because it is a lot! In fact, I've become convinced that the vast majority of us are juggling way more than we were designed to handle.

The question is this: What are we going to do about it?

Our Part to Play

So far in these pages, we've taken a deeper look into what stress is and why it's so corrosive in our lives. We've also explored the alternative to stress, which is for God to fill us with His peace—a peace that's beyond all comprehension.

Personally, I'm thankful that God is the source of the peace I need. If it were up to me to generate peace for myself, it would never happen. I wouldn't get anywhere close to living the abundant life I've experienced in recent years. In fact, trying to figure out a way to manufacture peace would probably make me feel stressed out!

Still, it's important for me to remember that I do have a part to play when it comes to passing the stress test and experiencing a stressless life. So do you. As we saw in the previous chapter, we can be filled with greater and deeper levels of God's peace when we know God, live in constant fellowship with Him, choose to be completely honest with

Him, and intentionally express thanksgiving to Him each and every day.

That's not all. You and I can also gain an advantage in the battle against stress by limiting the opportunities for stress to manifest itself in our lives. I said at the beginning of this book that we'll never remove every stressor from our lives, and that's absolutely true. However, we can remove *some* stressors—maybe even *a lot* of stressors. We can be proactive in limiting the threat that stress poses in our lives.

That's going to be our focus for the remaining chapters of this book. Specifically, we're going to examine six factors that are major causes of stress in the modern world: schedules, budgets, relationships, decisions, spiritual struggles, and circumstances that are beyond our control. These are some of the biggest balls we typically juggle as we make our way through life, which means that approaching these factors in the right way can significantly reduce the stressors we encounter and drastically increase our capacity for God's peace.

When it comes to our schedules—meaning the amount of time we have and our plan for spending it—there are many places in Scripture to find wisdom and guidance. But I think this passage stands out:

> Now as they were traveling along, [Jesus] entered a village; and a woman named Martha welcomed Him into her home. And she had a sister called Mary, who was also seated at the Lord's feet, and was listening to His word. But Martha was distracted with all her preparations; and she came up to Him and said, "Lord, do You not care that my sister has left me to do the serving by myself? Then

tell her to help me." But the Lord answered and said to her, "Martha, Martha, you are worried and distracted by many things; but only one thing is necessary; for Mary has chosen the good part, which shall not be taken away from her." (Luke 10:38–42)

Yes, we're going to spend some time talking about Mary and Martha. Now, I know a lot of pastors are tough on Martha when they preach about this story; it's easy to paint her as the villain and point out all the things she did wrong.

Personally, though, I have somewhat of a soft spot for Martha because she reminds me of myself. She and I are both doers. We like to get things done, and we like to keep a full plate. That's why this passage is so helpful in exploring how to approach our schedules in a way that reduces stressors and stress—because Martha is a reflection of our culture's drive to succeed, and Mary provides a great contrast with her central focus on Jesus.

As we work through this story, I'm going to ask you to consider three questions about your schedule. Fair warning: these aren't easy questions. They aren't the kind you can answer off the top of your head; you'll need to do some serious thinking. Also, these questions will likely be convicting—I know they are for me!

Here's the first one.

Does Your Schedule *Include* Time with Jesus, or Is It *Ordered around* Time with Jesus?

I encourage you to take a moment to think through this question. Chew on it a bit. When you look back over the last week, did your daily routine include some time with Jesus here and there, whenever you could fit it in? Or was time with Jesus the foundation of each day? What about over the past year? What about the past decade?

When we look at Luke 10, we see two very different attitudes toward the presence of Jesus.

First, the text says Martha "welcomed Him into her home." That word translated "welcomed" means to receive hospitably and kindly—to treat someone as a guest. So Jesus stopped by and Martha was willing to spend some time with Him. She made room for Him in her busy schedule, and she welcomed Him into her home.

Mary was different. The text says Mary was "seated at the Lord's feet, and was listening to His word." Do you see the difference there? In that culture, to sit at someone's feet was to recognize that person's authority and show respect. And the word translated "listening" means to hear with attention. When Jesus showed up, Mary stopped everything she was doing and gave Jesus her full attention.

It's interesting that Jesus's presence was part of Martha's plan. She was absolutely willing to include Him in her day. She was even willing to make Him one of her priorities. But Jesus's presence *was* Mary's plan. Jesus was her central priority in such a way that she ordered her day around Him.

Here's another way of looking at the contrast between these two women: if Martha had time, she was going to be with Jesus. Sadly, I'm afraid that's the way many of us approach our schedules as followers of Christ. We say, "Jesus, You're welcome to stop by—as long as I have the time." We build our schedules around what seems important to us and what we need to accomplish, and then we see if there's a way to fit in spending time in His presence.

Again, Mary was different. If Mary had time for nothing else, she was going to spend time with Jesus. She was willing to let everything else go—she was even willing to risk her sister's wrath—to place herself at Jesus's feet and give Him all her attention.

There's an exercise I've found useful when thinking through this subject. I'm going to give you a quote, and then I'll ask you to consider two questions about that quote.

Here's the quote from Henry Blackaby: "A love relationship with God is more important than any other single factor in your life."[2]

Now, here are the questions:

1. Do you believe that statement to be true?
2. Does your schedule reflect your answer to the question above?

If you're feeling convicted right now, I understand. And I want to make it clear that I'm not teaching these principles from the perspective of someone who gets this right all the time. I don't!

In fact, just this week I had one of those fifteen-hour days. You know the kind. The day was packed with meetings, and every meeting lasted longer than anticipated. I kept bouncing from conference room to office to conference room without feeling like I could catch my breath and gather my thoughts. On top of that, I was trying to resolve a conflict that kept running in the back of my mind all day. Plus, I had several notifications on my phone for unanswered texts and calls—and with each one, I felt the disappointment of letting someone else down.

Finally, my office hours came to an end. But this happened to be the day of our monthly meeting with our leadership team at the church. So I threw down some Chick-fil-A and walked straight into another meeting that lasted until 11:00 p.m. By the time I got home, I was done. Spent. Exhausted.

Right when I lay down, though, I sensed the still, small voice of the Holy Spirit say, "I sure missed you today." It wasn't a voice of harsh condemnation; it was a loving invitation. And in that moment, I realized, *I haven't spent any significant time with Jesus today*. I'd woken up late that morning and jumped headfirst into the gauntlet of the day in front of me and neglected the relationship that mattered the most.

However, I've consistently noticed that when I build my day around Jesus as my first priority, everything else falls into place. That doesn't mean I don't have problems or meetings or phone calls or conflicts. All that stuff is still there. But when my day is ordered around Jesus, I seem to respond to everything so much better because I'm filled with God's peace, and I have a firm understanding of what He wants me to accomplish.

> I've consistently noticed that when I build my day around Jesus as my first priority, everything else falls into place.

The reality is this: as a Jesus follower, you will never remove stress from your daily schedule until everything else in your day is ordered around time with Jesus. The other side of the coin is also true: as a Jesus follower, your daily schedule will never be saturated in God's peace until everything else in your day is ordered around time with Jesus. Time with Jesus ought to be the building block on which the rest of your day's activity is built.

How This Worked for Jesus

Before we jump to the second question for this chapter, let's take a look at what it means practically to build our schedules around time with Jesus. Thankfully, we can start by looking at how Jesus structured His own schedule. Here's something worth thinking about: no person in the history of the world has ever had more to accomplish than Jesus. Wouldn't you say that's true? Jesus's mission was so huge and so cosmically significant that no one else has ever come close—and yet it's also true that Jesus was never in a hurry.

Isn't that amazing? I challenge you to read through the Gospels and try to find a moment where Jesus was rushed—where Jesus had to hurry or play catch-up.

The reason Jesus was never in a hurry is because He lived His life in lockstep with the will of God the Father. He was perfectly aware of everything the Father wanted Him to accomplish each day. And, just as importantly, Jesus was perfectly aware of everything the Father wasn't interested in Him accomplishing.

How did Jesus know these things? Because He spent time daily with the Father. Look at what Jesus said in John 5:

> But He answered them, "My Father is working until now, and I Myself am working.". . . .
> "Truly, truly, I say to you, the Son can do nothing of Himself, unless it is something He sees the Father doing; for whatever

73

the Father does, these things the Son also does in the same way. For the Father loves the Son and shows Him all things that He Himself is doing; and the Father will show Him greater works than these, so that you will be amazed." (vv. 17, 19–20)

What was Jesus saying? First, God is working. God has specific plans and purposes He carries out each day, and He wants His children to be involved in those plans.

Second, Jesus was saying that His primary focus was to understand where the Father was working and how the Father wanted Him to join in His activity with His daily life. "For the Father loves the Son and shows Him all things that He Himself is doing." Jesus later told His disciples, "For I have come down from heaven, not to do My own will, but the will of Him who sent Me" (John 6:38).

Here's the reality: through His fellowship with the Father, Jesus ordered His life around that which He heard from the Father. How arrogant of us, then, to run out our door each day assuming we have a good handle on everything God wants us to do.

How This Works for Us

We realized a dream at Hope Church near the end of 2020 when we put the final touches on our brand-new worship center. We'd been at full capacity in multiple services in our old worship center for years, but we still had a lot of room on our campus grounds. So we built the new facility just a couple hundred feet from my office—which meant I got to go out and view the construction site a couple of times a week. I was like a kid in a candy store as I witnessed each progressive step of that building going up.

One of the elements of construction that impressed me most was the foundation. I knew foundations were important, of course, but I didn't fully understand the enormity of such an undertaking. For this building, various crews spent weeks digging a massive hole. They filled 590 dump trucks with dirt, clay, and bedrock. Then the crews coordinated over four hundred truckloads of concrete in order to place a foundation that weighed over eight million pounds!

I remember watching truck after truck drive in to fill the different forms of that foundation with cement. I thought, *Nothing could ever shake this building loose.* Why? Because the foundation was so secure.

That's what I mean when I talk about building our schedules around spending time in fellowship with Jesus. What I don't mean is spending our entire day with Jesus. I don't mean we isolate ourselves in a cave somewhere and do nothing but spend time with Jesus. We have families, we have to work, and we have other things we need to do. More importantly, we have lots of critical work God desires to do through us in order to bring Him glory and accomplish His mission.

Building our schedule around time with Jesus means making Him the foundation of our schedule. Of our day. Of our week. Of our year. Of our entire lives. And it all starts with actively, intentionally making spending time with Jesus the most important part of our day, and then adding everything else around and on top of that critical priority.

My point is this: time alone with Jesus isn't just a good thing we should do for our spiritual life. It's not simply an emotional pick-me-up that will help get us through the day. If we want to remove stressors and stress from our schedule, and if we want to fully open ourselves to be filled with

God's unshakable peace, we need to make spending time with Jesus the central component of our schedule each and every day.

Now, here's the second question.

Is Your Schedule Dictated by What's Urgent, or Is It Designed to Accomplish What's Important?

You've probably heard people talk about "the tyranny of the urgent." Unfortunately, as we look back at our story, it's clear that Martha was a victim of that tyranny—at least during this encounter with Jesus. Let's look back at the text: "But Martha was distracted with all her preparations; and she came up to Him and said, 'Lord, do You not care that my sister has left me to do the serving by myself? Then tell her to help me'" (Luke 10:40).

Did you notice that Martha had the guts to give Jesus a command? You don't see that often in Scripture! More to the point, she allowed her schedule to be dictated by what was urgent rather than by what was most important.

Again, I feel for Martha here because she was intent on getting things accomplished. She was the hostess. She was the workhorse. She was the one entrusted to make sure everything was finished the right way and finished on time—and yet she'd lost one of her workers. "My sister has left me to do the serving by myself."

Martha's problem was that she didn't allow herself any space to determine priorities. She allowed her time to be dominated by whatever was in front of her—whatever fires needed to be put out in a given moment—rather than stepping back to evaluate the best way for her time to be spent.

In other words, Martha assumed responsibility for whatever needed to get done around her.

Jesus's answer to Martha's command is powerful: "Martha, Martha, you are worried and distracted by many things; but only one thing is necessary; for Mary has chosen the good part, which shall not be taken away from her" (vv. 41–42).

Mary had designed her schedule to accomplish what was most important. She knew everything that needed to get done in order to prepare a meal for Jesus and His disciples. She understood all the chores. All the tasks. I'm sure Mary even had a pretty good idea that Martha would be displeased if she abandoned her assignments—yet she abandoned them anyway. Why? Because she understood that Jesus was more important.

I want to look at that word *chosen* for a minute. Jesus said Mary had "chosen the good part." In the original language, that term means "to select from many options." It carries the idea of having lots of things in front of you, and then making an intentional selection based on a specific preference.

To illustrate this concept, I'll share something. Sometimes my wife asks me to run to the grocery store and pick up a few items. Now, that doesn't happen much anymore, because over the course of our marriage, she's learned I always take three times longer than she expects, I call her about a dozen times to ask a bunch of questions, and I usually come home with a whole mess of things she didn't ask me to get. Despite all that, very occasionally, and with a limited amount of cash in my pocket, Kristie will sometimes ask me to go to the store for a specific number of items.

Steak is a good example because she knows how much I enjoy a nice steak dinner. When I get to the meat counter to buy steak for my family, it's serious business. It's an investment of my time and attention. I don't just grab whatever is freshest or cheapest. No, I work my way through each available option. I pick up those packages and examine them like an archaeologist scrutinizing a newfound fossil. Why? Because I'm trying to choose the very best cut of meat!

That's how Jesus described Mary in this story. She had "chosen the good part," and it wouldn't be taken away from her. Mary had chosen what was best because she intentionally structured her day to accomplish what was important rather than being bullied by what was urgent.

You might be thinking, *That makes sense, Vance, but how do I know what's most important? How do I set up the right priorities?*

Great question, and the answer goes back to question one from earlier in this chapter. The only way to establish the right priorities in our lives—to accurately determine what's most important—is to figure out what God has chosen to be most important. And the only way to figure that out is by intentionally making Him the foundation of our schedules.

See how it works? When we make spending time with Jesus our first priority, we gain a better understanding of what's important in our lives, which means we can resist the pull of what's merely urgent.

Jesus gave us a great example of how this process works in the Gospel of Mark. To set the scene a little, this was early in Jesus's public ministry. He arrived in the town of Capernaum, along with Peter and Andrew, His new disciples, and immediately began teaching in the synagogue. Jesus taught with power, cast out demons, and then retired to Peter's home, where He healed Peter's mother-in-law of a dangerous fever. It's not surprising that by this time the townspeople were seriously impressed with Jesus. The text says, "When evening came, after the sun had set, they began bringing to Him all who were ill and those who were demon-possessed. And the whole city had gathered at the door. And He healed many who were ill with various diseases, and cast out many demons; and He would not permit the demons to speak, because they knew who He was" (Mark 1:32–34).

Now, as a pastor, this is just about as good as it gets. Jesus had done incredible things, and the whole town was lined up outside His door just to see Him and hear from Him. They were eating out of His hand! What a perfect time to establish a church, start raising some funds, and really get His ministry off the ground. Right?

That's not what happened.

And in the early morning, while it was still dark, Jesus got up, left the house, and went away to a secluded place, and prayed there for a time. Simon and his companions eagerly searched for Him; and they found Him and said to Him, "Everyone is looking for You." He said to them, "Let's go somewhere else to the towns nearby, so that I may also preach there; for this is why I came." And He went into their synagogues preaching throughout Galilee, and casting out the demons. (vv. 35–39)

Here's a question: Would it have been a bad thing for Jesus to stay in that town, keep healing those people, and continue to teach them about God's plan for their lives? No.

Jesus spent a lot of His public ministry teaching, healing, and driving out demons. Also, can you sense the urgency in the situation? The people were so desperate for more of Jesus that they "eagerly searched for Him" early in the morning. They wanted more!

So why didn't Jesus stay? The answer is that, while remaining in Capernaum wasn't a bad option, it wasn't the *best* option. Why? Because it wasn't the Father's will—it didn't line up with the Father's plan. And how did Jesus know what was included in the Father's plan? Because He intentionally set aside time to spend with the Father. Therefore, Jesus was able to accomplish what was most important rather than being pushed and pulled by whatever was urgent.

> If you want to reduce the number of stressors that bombard you each day, and if you want your schedule to be saturated in God's peace, you need to intentionally build that schedule to accomplish what's important rather than be dictated by what's urgent.

Here's the reality for you and me: when it comes to our schedules, every time we say yes to something, we're saying no to a whole lot of other somethings. We better be sure, then, that what we say yes to is more important than what we say no to.

If you want to reduce the number of stressors that bombard you each day, and if you want your schedule to be saturated in God's peace, you need to intentionally build that schedule to accomplish what's important rather than be dictated by what's urgent.

Let's move to the third and final question for this chapter.

Does Your Schedule Express a Heart *Captivated* by What's Eternally Significant, or Is It *Distracted* by What's Temporary?

Looking back at Luke 10, I'd like to highlight some important words before we move on from Mary and Martha. First, verse 40 says Martha "was distracted with all her preparations." And later Jesus told her, "Martha, Martha, you are worried and distracted by many things" (v. 41).

Worried and distracted. Distracted and worried. That sounds like us, doesn't it? That sounds like what we often think of as the modern world, with our phones, our iPads, our social media accounts, and our never-ending list of movies and TV shows we need to catch. Martha would have fit in great in our society. The question is, What are we so worried about and distracted by? In my experience, not much.

For example, take a moment to consider these questions:

- What did you have for dinner four days ago?
- What (if anything) got accomplished at the last meeting you attended for work?
- Who read or responded to the Christmas cards you sent out last year?
- How many of the birthday presents you received on your last birthday are you still using today?
- What were some of the most important emails you wrote last week?
- How many likes did your Facebook post get last Tuesday?

Kudos to you if you can actually answer any of those questions with any clarity. I can't. But I hope you see my point: so much of what fills up our time and attracts our attention each day is ultimately meaningless. Insignificant. Temporary. Of course, our culture itself is a big part of the problem. We live in a materialistic society. That means some of the brightest minds in the world are spending billions of dollars every year with the specific goal of pushing you to spend more and more of your resources on more and more stuff so you can be more and more entertained, which then causes you to desire more and more pleasure, which is why you spend more and more time trying to earn more and more resources so you can buy more and more stuff—and the cycle goes on.

Let me show you what God said about that cycle: "Do not love the world nor the things in the world. If anyone loves the world, the love of the Father is not in him. For all that is in the world, the lust of the flesh and the lust of the eyes and the boastful pride of life, is not from the Father, but is from the world" (1 John 2:15–16).

Now, if you stopped reading right there, you might think, *This is God trying to stop me from having fun. This is God trying to rob me of the joys and the pleasures I can find in the world just because He wants all the attention to be on Him.* Many people think this way. But look at the next verse: "The world is passing away and also its lusts; but the one who does the will of God continues to live forever" (v. 17).

The truth is, God isn't trying to rob you of joy. He's not trying to steal your fun or take away your level of comfort. God is trying to be honest with you. This is Him saying, "Yes, you can love all that stuff, but it's fleeting—it doesn't last."

You and I know that to be true, don't we? If you've spent part of your life chasing money, you know money doesn't solve all your problems. If you've spent your life chasing power, you know there's always someone more powerful—always another level you have to reach. If you've spent your life chasing pleasure, you know that the next thrill is never as good as the last thrill; you're always chasing more.

Do you see why it's so easy to be stressed in today's world? We're chasing after a bunch of stuff God never intended us to chase. We're pursuing a life defined by what's temporary rather than what's eternal. And it causes distraction. It causes worry. It causes stress.

Thankfully, there's a better way. We can make the same choice as Mary and live our lives in pursuit of that which will never be taken away: our connection to Jesus. Our work in His kingdom. Our joy in eternal life.

Five Steps You Can Take

Before I wrap up this chapter, I want to get really practical. I want to show you five steps you can take to significantly remove stressors from your schedule—and therefore significantly increase your ability to receive and enjoy God's peace.

Step 1: Establish your daily rhythm with Jesus. The first thing you can do to remove stress from your schedule is to establish a daily rhythm of spending significant, uninterrupted time with Jesus.

I know the question you're probably thinking right now: *Do I have to spend time with Jesus in the morning?* I get that question all the time, and many Christians believe the only real way to be effective in your devotions or "God time" is to make them the first thing you do each day.

Here's my opinion: be intentional about setting aside whatever time will be most effective and conducive for your relationship with Him. That might be the morning. That might be the evening. It might even be both! You might need to set aside small pockets of time throughout the day to really maintain your sense of intimacy with Jesus and your awareness of what He wants to accomplish in and through you that day.

Remember, Jesus is a Person. He's not a book or a machine. So, determine whatever times work best to deepen your relationship with Christ as a Person, and then be ruthless in maintaining that rhythm each day.

Step 2: Determine what's most important in your life. I'm talking about priorities. Your core values. What elements of your life are most important?

If figuring that out sounds overwhelming, I understand. But the truth is, you can't hit a target you're not aiming for. Meaning, you won't build your schedule around what's most important unless you understand what's most important. You have to take whatever time is necessary to think this through.

Actually, don't just think this through; pray it through. You need to hear from your heavenly Father. Get a clear sense of what He wants you to accomplish and pursue through your time. It's also a good idea to seek out wise counsel from those who know you best. What does your spouse see as your biggest gifts and opportunities? How would your closest friends describe your core values?

Lastly, make sure you're thinking through biblical priorities and values—not what the world wants you to focus on

Running Out of Time

or commit yourself to. The goal here is to identify the core priorities that will lead you to abundant life, then structure your schedule to elevate those core priorities rather than allow them to be buried under the stress, worry, and distractions of everyday life.

Here's a great quote from a pastor I knew personally: "God's great gift to you, number one, is Jesus, and number two, is time. God has given you time to work, time to serve, time to love, time to laugh, time to labor; but, like any gift, how you use it is really up to you. And we need to see every day—this day and every day—as a gift from God."[3]

Step 3: Build a plan for your daily life around what's most important. This is where the rubber really starts to hit the road. When you have a regular and healthy connection with Jesus, you'll gain understanding about what's important in life. And when you know what's most important, you can intentionally structure each day to focus primarily on those concerns.

Here's a practical example from my life. I've been married to Kristie for thirty years. Obviously our marriage is a huge priority in my life. Next to Jesus, my relationship with my wife is the most important relationship in my life. Therefore, Kristie and I have put together a plan to make sure our marriage is valued and supported within our schedule.

Here's that plan in a nutshell:

- We pray together daily.
- We date together weekly.
- We escape together monthly, which is a full day where we just enjoy each other's company.

85

- We get away together quarterly, which means we travel somewhere overnight or for a weekend.
- We retreat together annually, which means we spend several nights away together to review the past year and plan for what's coming.

That's a practical example of a plan for daily life to elevate what's important. I'm not recommending that every marriage be structured this way, but it works well for Kristie and me.

Here's the reality: if you have more on your schedule than you can realistically accomplish in a day, then there are things on your schedule God didn't put there. More to the point, there are things on your schedule God doesn't want there. How do I know that's true? Because we've already seen that trying to handle more than our resources can bear will produce stress—and stress has never been part of God's plan for our lives.

Step 4: Create margin within your plan for God's activity in the lives of others. This is something I learned relatively late in my life. It used to be that I would pack my schedule as full as possible. If I found an extra thirty seconds lying around during a day, I was going to make full use of that time and cram in an extra thing to do.

Not anymore. I've learned the value of having margin in my life and in my schedule.

If you're not familiar with that term, *margin* is the "white space" of our lives. It's the time we leave in our schedule for unexpected moments or unplanned events. Building margin into your schedule simply means not planning out every moment of your day. You need to leave some space for God to do the unexpected.

To give you an example of what I mean, just look at the Gospels. You'll see that Jesus was often interrupted, but He was never off course from God's agenda. Think about all the times Jesus was interrupted in Scripture. He was walking in one direction and a woman touched his cloak so she could be healed. He was walking toward another town and a servant rushed up with an urgent request.

He was walking down a mountain and a father pulled Him aside to deal with a demon that was trying to kill his son.

Do you see what I mean? Jesus was interrupted all the time, but those interruptions never interfered with His agenda. Why? Because He left margin in His schedule.

Step 5: Establish accountability to eliminate distractions. I know from experience that I need people in my life who are willing and able to make sure I'm following the plan I've heard from God. When

> If you have more on your schedule than you can realistically accomplish in a day, then there are things on your schedule God didn't put there. More to the point, there are things on your schedule God doesn't want there.

I spend time with God and He shows me what's important, I need people checking my schedule and my life to make sure my actions reflect those realities.

I believe the same is true for you. Because it's a lot easier to wreck a good thing than it is to build one. You need some safety nets to make sure your schedule doesn't go downhill.

Speaking very practically once more, I meet regularly with two people who ask me tough questions about the things I've told them are important based on what God has communicated to me. They ask me, "How's your time with your wife? Are you following your plan for making her a priority?" They ask about my kids. They ask about my discipling relationships.

Why do I allow those questions? Why do I encourage them? Because I want to continue living an abundant life—a stressless life. And I don't want to allow any opportunities for unnecessary stressors to blossom into the kind of fearful concern that will harm me and create stress.

What about you? I've given you three questions to consider in this chapter. Like I said before, they're not easy questions. I hope you've been wrestling with them, and I hope you'll continue to do so in the days and weeks to come. Because when you remove unnecessary stressors from your schedule, you open yourself to everything God desires for you to experience—including the fullness of His peace.

4

Making Ends Meet

How Do I Find God's Peace in My Budget?

Charles Calvin was hoping for good news when he stopped by the ATM during his lunch break. What he found went way beyond his wildest dreams.

A fireman, Charles was due to receive a $1,700 stimulus payment from the government because of the COVID-19 pandemic. After making a small withdrawal from the ATM, he looked at the bottom of the receipt to see whether the money had finally been deposited into his account. That's when his jaw hit the floor.

The receipt showed an account balance of 8.2 million dollars.

His first thought was, *What in the world is going on here?* His second thought was to show the receipt to the captain of his firehouse and get some advice on what to do next.

A little skeptical of his friend's good fortune, the captain encouraged Charles to return to the ATM and double-check his math. They went together, and Charles fed his card into the machine. Sure enough, there was the bank balance of 8.2 million dollars. The captain had Charles try again, and he got the same result.

Sadly, when Charles called his bank the next day to get some answers, they informed him the clerical error had been fixed and the money was no longer present in his account. But the teller did offer some good news: his $1,700 stimulus payment had come through.

"It kind of stinks," Charles later reflected. "You go from being a millionaire on paper one second, then back to being broke again. But I guess once you're poor, you ain't got nowhere else to go but up."[1]

I like that attitude! What Charles said is true for a lot of people in today's world, and I believe his experience points to an even larger truth: money is stressful. In fact, money is one of the biggest stressors in our lives.

According to the "Stress in America 2020" report from the American Psychological Association, the overall performance of the economy is a significant source of stress for 63 percent of Americans, and 64 percent of adults say money is a major source of stress in their personal lives. That number jumps to 73 percent for adults with a household income under $50,000,[2] which is significant because four in ten American households are in that category.[3]

But financial stress doesn't just impact us as individuals—it hits our families as well. Scholarly studies have shown that financial stress among couples is by far the top predictor of whether those couples will get divorced.[4] Another study offered this frightening conclusion: "Children assume the fear of losing the family home and the trepidation of getting the bills paid on time as they observe their parents struggling to stay in the black. This stress is often revealed as moody behavior, increased anger or aggression, inexplicable illness, or poor academic performance."[5]

Why Are We So Stressed about Money?

When I see these kinds of statistics, the big question that comes to my mind is why. Why are people in our culture so stressed about money?

Or, to use the terms we've been emphasizing in these pages, why is money such a significant stressor in our lives? And why does that particular stressor so often develop into full-blown stress?

We're going to explore four specific answers to those questions, and we're going to do so by focusing on some important passages from God's Word. Before we jump to Scripture, however, let me say one thing. I know people often use the Bible as a club—especially pastors. It's easy for someone like me to point out a Scripture passage and say, "Look at all the ways you're messing up." It's easy for someone like you to feel beaten over the head with all the things God says you're supposed to do and all the ways you're not doing them.

The truth is that God's Word is neither a club nor a finger pointed in accusation. Instead, James 1 says the Bible is a mirror. It's something that allows us to take an honest look at ourselves and see what's really going on.

I use a mirror every day. We have a full-size one in our bathroom, and I stand in front of it every day after I go through my routine of showering, shaving, getting dressed, and so on. Why do I stand in front of the mirror? To get a good look at myself. Specifically, to see if anything is out of place and needs to be fixed. Maybe my hair needs some work. Maybe my clothes don't match as well as I thought they would. Maybe there's a stain on my pants I hadn't noticed. The mirror reveals it all with brutal honesty.

That's the same spirit in which I teach principles out of God's Word. I hold up the Scriptures as a mirror—not for me to offer judgments or criticisms but for you to look into and decide for yourself whether anything is out of place.

Of course, if anything is out of place, the good news is that it can be fixed. You can eliminate many of the stressors our society produces because of its obsession with money, and you can significantly reduce the opportunities for money troubles or money worries to devolve into stress. As Charles Calvin so rightly put it, "You ain't got nowhere else to go but up."

Having said all that, let's explore four reasons why so many people in our culture are stressed out because of money.

We Have a Lack of Contentment

The book of 1 Timothy is a letter written by the apostle Paul to a young leader in the early church. Paul was Timothy's mentor, and he appointed Timothy as the leader of one of the churches he'd planted during his missionary journeys. Paul offered important advice to both Timothy and the members of his church, and some of his most practical guidance was on this subject of money and finances.

Let's start with 1 Timothy 6:6–8: "But godliness *actually* is a means of great gain when accompanied by contentment.

For we have brought nothing into the world, so we cannot take anything out of it, either. If we have food and covering, with these we shall be content" (emphasis added).

Right off the bat, Paul puts his finger on the antidote for those who are stressing out about money. That antidote is *contentment*. When we're able to be content with our circumstances—especially the state of our finances—we'll no longer be crushed and squeezed by stress related to money.

Here's the problem: our definition of contentment is based on an enormous lie. For decades now, Western culture has pushed the idea that contentment is found in getting everything we want. Most people today believe they will feel content when they finally receive or have access to all the things they want. This applies to material possessions, of course, but it also means getting everything we want in terms of relationships, career, purpose, power, success, and so on. *When I finally have all that at my fingertips, I will be content.*

The reality is that there's always more to want.

I recently had an epiphany on this topic while I was watching my grandchildren play in our pool. That's their favorite thing to do whenever they come over to our place, and their second favorite thing to do is try to convince Kristie and me to jump in with them—which is a pretty easy goal for them to achieve.

Kristie keeps a bunch of pool toys at our house for such occasions, including a cup that has a hole in the bottom. My granddaughter Karis has a special attachment to this cup. She'll sit on the side of the pool and scoop water into the cup, then hold it up and watch the water drain out the bottom in trickles and drops. She does it over and over again: Scoop, lift, and drain. Scoop, lift, and drain.

My epiphany came as I was watching her drain the water from the cup for the hundredth time. I noticed the amount draining from the cup changed depending on how much she scooped in there to start with. When only a little bit of water was in the cup, it would leak slowly from the hole in the bottom—drip, drip, drip. But, when the cup was full, the water would rush out in a stream.

That's when it hit me: our culture's approach to contentment is a cup with a hole in the bottom. The more we fill our lives with possessions, status, and all the things we believe money can buy, the faster it all drains away—and the faster we feel empty once again.

Time magazine once published an article by Gregg Easterbrook called "The Real Truth about Money." The whole article is fascinating, but this quote in particular caught my attention:

> If you made a graph of American life since the end of World War II, every line concerning money and the things that money can buy would soar upward, a statistical monument to materialism.
>
> Inflation-adjusted income per American household has tripled. The size of the typical new house has more than doubled. A two-car garage was once a goal; now we're nearly a three-car nation. Designer everything, personal electronics and other items that didn't even exist a half-century ago are now affordable. No matter how you chart the trends in earning and spending, everything is up, up, up.
>
> But if you made a chart of American happiness since World War II, the lines would be as flat as a marble tabletop.[6]

Do you see the problem? We've been told over and over that buying the latest thing or reaching a new goal will bring us happiness and contentment. But even as we buy more and achieve more, we don't get happier. Eventually the disconnect between what we think will happen and what actually happens becomes a major stressor. We're pouring water into a cup with a hole in the bottom, and the result is stress.

Looking back at 1 Timothy 6, it's clear Paul had very different ideas when it comes to money: "For we have brought nothing into the world, so we cannot take anything out of it, either" (v. 7). Oh, if only we could grasp that truth! If only we could see the freedom it offers.

Then Paul gives his own definition of contentment in verse 8: "If we have food and covering, with these we shall be content." In other words, contentment isn't based on getting everything we want—it's based on having our needs met. *What's the difference?* you ask. I've always defined those two terms this way: a *need* is something that makes life possible; a *want* is something that makes life easier.

We must understand that contentment is a choice. When our basic needs have been satisfied—I'm talking about food, clothing, shelter, and purpose—we have the opportunity to choose contentment. To embrace contentment. The alternative is to shift our focus from needs to wants, which will lead us down the rabbit hole of never having enough and never being content.

Here's the truth: there's nothing wrong with pursuing a good living and enjoying the wants we receive. But if we're not content with what we *do* have, we won't be content when we get what we *don't* have. And that's exactly why lack of contentment is a key source of stress.

We Have a Love of Money

Our lives become even more stress filled when we combine a passive lack of contentment with an active love of money. That's a dangerous combination.

Look back at what Paul said in 1 Timothy 6: "But those who want to get rich fall into temptation and a trap, and many foolish and harmful desires which plunge people into ruin and destruction. For the love of money is a root of all sorts of evil, and some by longing for it have wandered away from the faith and pierced themselves with many griefs" (vv. 9–10).

Have you seen people plunged into ruin and destruction because they were chasing after money? Me too. It happens to celebrities, it happens within businesses, it happens within our local communities, and it happens within our churches.

> There's nothing wrong with pursuing a good living and enjoying the wants we receive. But if we're not content with what we **do** have, we won't be content when we get what we **don't** have.

To love money this way means that you're willing to go to any lengths to obtain more of it—and not just cash but also all the things money is supposed to be able to buy. It means your identity is wrapped up in material wealth. Instead of defining yourself by who you are in Christ, your identity is based on what you have (or don't have).

Does that describe you? Do you consistently need to have the best? The newest car. The latest technology. The biggest house. Again, I don't ask these questions as an accusation;

rather, I'm holding up the mirror of God's Word and asking you to evaluate yourself. Are you stressed out because you have a love of money?

Ultimately, the tragedy is that, when we pursue a love of money, we choose to heap stress on our own heads. Paul says such people have "pierced themselves with many griefs" (1 Tim. 6:10).

We Don't Manage Our Money by God's Design

The third reason so many people are stressed out by money is that they fail to manage their money in a way that lines up with God's plans, specifically God's plans for our money.

Look again at Paul's instructions to Timothy: "But flee from these things, you man of God, and pursue righteousness, godliness, faith, love, perseverance, and gentleness" (v. 11). Talk about dramatic!

There are two imperatives in that verse. Two commands. The first is to flee. Paul told Timothy—and by extension all Jesus followers—to "flee from these things." Which things? The lack of contentment and the love of money. Remember back in Genesis 39 when Joseph was tempted by Potiphar's wife and he fled so quickly that he left his coat in her hands? Paul was using the same language and the same idea when speaking to Timothy. He said, "Don't let those things even get close to you. Run away!"

The second command is to pursue. Paul commanded us to "pursue righteousness, godliness, faith, love, perseverance, and gentleness."

The whole idea here is that God has plans for our lives. He has a design for the world and for history as a whole, and He has a design for each of us living in the world and living in history as individuals. Paul wanted us to see that one particular direction is harmful to us and not part of God's plan, so we should flee from it. The other direction is beneficial to us because it is part of God's plan, which means we should pursue it.

Here's the truth we often miss: God's design for our lives includes our finances. His plan includes what we do with our money. That's clear when we jump down to verses 17–19:

> Instruct those who are rich in this present world not to be conceited or to set their hope on the uncertainty of riches, but on God, who richly supplies us with all things to enjoy. Instruct them to do good, to be rich in good works, to be generous and ready to share, storing up for themselves the treasure of a good foundation for the future, so that they may take hold of that which is truly life.

What we need to understand is that our money isn't really ours. Scripture says it's God "who richly supplies us with all things." The resources we possess ultimately belong to God, and He has given them to us for a purpose. We are His stewards, and He intends for us to use His resources according to His plan.

What is that plan? It's unique for each individual and each household, but it generally includes remaining "rich in good works," being "generous and ready to share," and building "a good foundation for the future" (we'll talk about budgeting in a moment).

Here's the rub: when we break away from God's design for our money—whether intentionally or unintentionally, consciously or in ignorance—we bring stressors down upon ourselves. Why? Because we're not pursuing what's best.

The question is simple: Are you pursuing God's design with the resources He's given you, or are you following your own plan? If it's the latter, you will experience stress.

We're in the Middle of Something beyond Our Control

The first three reasons we get stressed out by money are because we have a lack of contentment, we possess a love of money, and we fail to manage our resources according to God's design. All three of those have one thing in common: us. The choices we make produce the stress.

However, it's certainly true that sometimes—maybe even often—the reason we become stressed out by money doesn't involve our choices. So, the fourth reason for why money can be so stressful is that we're caught up in something beyond our control.

Do you remember Elijah from the Old Testament? He was a prophet who was involved in a whole bunch of miracles and explosive confrontations with evil kings. But one moment from Elijah's life is especially helpful in understanding this topic of being caught in the middle of a situation we can't control.

Here's how it started:

Now Elijah the Tishbite, who was of the settlers of Gilead, said to Ahab, "As the LORD, the God of Israel lives, before whom I stand, there shall certainly be neither dew nor rain during these years, except by my word." Then the word of the LORD came to him, saying, "Go away from here and turn eastward, and hide yourself by the brook Cherith, which is east of the Jordan. And it shall be that you will drink from the brook, and I have commanded the ravens to provide food for you there." (1 Kings 17:1–4)

Personally, I don't know what kind of food ravens had access to back in Elijah's day, but I bet they weren't bringing him hamburgers. Still, this was Elijah demonstrating faith in God's provision. He had the ravens bringing food, and he had the brook for water, so everything was good. No need for stress. Right?

Well, here's what happened next: "But it happened after a while that the brook dried up, because there was no rain in the land" (v. 7).

What? That's not fair! Elijah was doing exactly what God had told him to do. He was in exactly the place God had told him to be. And he still had to endure difficulty?

When has the brook dried up for you? It could be the loss of a job. It could be the medical bill (or, more likely, the stack of medical bills) that wiped out everything you'd saved. It could be a lawsuit. It could even be the blessing of a new child that also includes a bunch of new expenses you didn't plan for.

The reality is that we all get caught up in financial troubles beyond our control. But here's the truth I want you to consider: *those troubles are not beyond God's control.* He is still sovereign, He still loves you and wants what's best for you, and He still has the ability to bring about what's best in your life.

That's what happened to Elijah. When the brook dried up, God instructed His prophet to break camp and find a widow in the town of Zarephath who would provide for him. To make a long story short, through God's provision and power, Elijah and this widow experienced miracles and were able to provide for one another in mutually encouraging ways—a win-win.

The same thing happens in our lives when we trust God in the face of difficult moments. In fact, God often allows the brook to dry up in our lives precisely because He has something better in store for us—something He intends as a vehicle to reveal His glory, bless us in new ways, and expand His kingdom.

Good News about Money

It's time to look in the mirror once more. Are you stressed about money? Are stressors piling up because of finances, bills, the economy in general, or your specific situation?

If so, chances are good that those stressors can be traced to one of these four things:

1. You have a lack of contentment.
2. You have a love of money.
3. You're not managing your money by God's design.
4. You're in the middle of something beyond your control.

Here's the good news: no matter why you're feeling stressed out by money, there's hope. There's a way to remove many of the stressors that are piling up on your shoulders. And there's a way to be filled with God's peace regarding your money so that whatever stressors remain don't devolve into stress.

We're going to explore that hope for the rest of this chapter, and it all starts with these words of Jesus from His Sermon on the Mount:

For this reason I say to you, do not be worried about your life, as to what you will eat or what you will drink; nor for your body, as to what you will put on. Is life not more than food, and the body more than clothing? Look at the birds of the sky, that they do not sow, nor reap, nor gather crops into barns, and yet your heavenly Father feeds them. Are you not much more important than they? And which of you by worrying can add a single day to his life's span? And why are you worried about clothing? Notice how the lilies of the field grow; they do not labor nor do they spin thread for cloth, yet I say to you that not even Solomon in all his glory clothed himself like one of these. But if God so clothes the grass of the field, which is alive today and to-morrow is thrown into the furnace, will He not much more clothe you? You of little faith! Do not worry then, saying, "What are we to eat?" or "What are we to drink?" or "What are we to wear for clothing?" For the Gentiles eagerly seek all these things; for your heavenly Father knows that you need all these things. But seek first His kingdom and His righteousness, and all these things will be provided to you. (Matt. 6:25–33)

Whew! I know that's quite a few verses, but there's a lot of truth and freedom packed into that passage.

First things first. What did Jesus mean when He said, "For this reason . . ." (v. 25)? Well, He had already been talking about money during His sermon. He had already told His hearers not to store up treasures on earth, but instead to store up treasures in heaven. Why? Because "where your treasure is, there your heart will be also" (v. 21). Jesus had already taught that no person can serve two masters, which means we have to choose between God and money.

With all that in the background, He said, "For this reason I say to you" (v. 25), meaning the verses above are Jesus's solution to the problem of money. The principles in those verses are Jesus's solution to the problem of money causing so much stress in our lives.

> When I honor God with my finances, I can trust Him to satisfy all my needs.

We're going to unpack those verses in the pages to come, but first I want to summarize what Jesus said as a single principle—that way you can keep it in mind as you work through the entire passage.

Here's the principle: *When I honor God with my finances, I can trust Him to satisfy all my needs.* That's the core of what Jesus wants us to understand about money and the stress it can produce in our lives.

Are you ready to dig in? We're going to finish this chapter by exploring that principle in two sections: how to honor God with our finances and how to trust Him to satisfy our needs.

How to Honor God with Your Finances

A few years back, a friend of mine from Las Vegas gave me a very special gift. It was a Navy SEAL-issued SIG Sauer P226. I didn't know much about the weapon at the time, but after some research, I learned that this particular handgun is exclusive to the Navy SEAL teams within the US military. When I learned that, I was amazed by my friend's generosity!

I grew up in the gun-loving South, but I haven't had much experience with guns since I moved to Las Vegas decades ago. So the P226 sat on a shelf in my closet for a few years until I told another friend about it who is very experienced with firearms. He offered to take me out to a gun range to try out my gift.

You know what I learned from that experience? I really need a target.

Some people like to go out in the middle of nowhere and just blow stuff up. They like the power and the noise and the impact of shooting, all in a controlled environment. I'm not that way. What I enjoy on a shooting range is narrowing my focus and concentrating on a target—concentrating on that singular goal—before pulling the trigger.

I want to offer you a similar opportunity as we explore how to honor God with our finances. Specifically, I want to give you a target to aim for. Under normal circumstances, when aiming at a target, we all aim for the bull's-eye. What I want you to understand is that the bull's-eye for honoring God with your finances actually has three layers, and it's only when each of these layers is being fleshed out in our lives that we can honestly say we're hitting the target. If we could double-click on the exact bull's-eye of what it looks like to honor God with our finances, we'd find these three layers:

- The center of the target is giving to the Lord.
- The next layer is saving for the future.
- The final layer is budgeting to live.

Those three layers are what it looks like to hit the bull's-eye of honoring God with our money. Now, this isn't just theory. This target is based on decades of seeking the Lord and partnering with my wife to manage our own finances and our own household. We've experienced God's unshakable

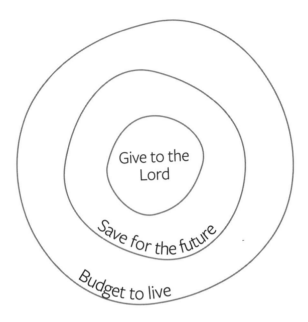

peace in the financial matters of our lives in ways that have blown us away. Moreover, I've learned to trust this target after decades of teaching these principles in the church God has called me to shepherd and watching God bring indescribable peace into the lives of everyday people hitting this target.

Let's explore each layer of the target in greater detail.

Give to the Lord

Looking back at Matthew 6, it's clear that Jesus knows how big of a deal money is in our lives. He talked about the issues that constantly press on our minds and keep us up at night—our food, our clothes, how we're going to provide for our families, what kind of home we can set up.

Jesus is aware of our needs and our desires. And you know what He said about them? "Your heavenly Father knows that

105

you need all these things. But seek first His kingdom and His righteousness, and all these things will be provided to you" (vv. 32–33).

Here's the principle: if you want to take a step toward a stressless life when it comes to money, start by actively and intentionally giving to the Lord. Make that the very first thing you do—the very center of what you aim for with your resources.

> If you want to take a step toward a stressless life when it comes to money, start by actively and intentionally giving to the Lord.

Right now you might be thinking, *That doesn't make any sense.* You're not the only one who says that! People argue with me all the time when I teach this principle. They say, "Vance, I am neck-deep in debt" or, "Vance, I just lost my job, and I don't know how I'm going to put food on the table for my kids—and you're telling me the way I can find peace is by taking what money I do have and giving it to God?"

Yes. That's what I'm saying, and I know it doesn't make a lot of sense to most people. Most people respond to money trouble and stress by focusing on themselves. They try to make sure all their bases are covered, and all their needs are met by figuring out what resources they have and applying them to those needs. That makes sense in our culture.

Here's the problem: focusing on themselves is probably what got those people into money trouble in the first place.

Jesus wants you to take a different approach. He said the Father knows your situation. The Father knows how many mouths you have to feed. The Father knows all the bills that are coming your way. The Father knows how much less you're making than you used to make. Therefore, Jesus said, "Seek first His kingdom."

By the way, this concept didn't originate with Jesus. It's present throughout the whole Bible. The book of Proverbs, for example, says it this way:

> Honor the LORD from your wealth,
> And from the first of all your produce. (3:9)

That word *first* means to choose what's best—the choicest part.

Here's the principle from God's Word: out of everything you receive as income, you are to give *first* to the mission of God in the world. You are to "seek first His kingdom." That means you don't take care of yourself first and then use whatever is left over to honor God. No, it means you give God what is first and best, and then you'll be amazed at what is left over to care for your needs.

How does that work? Giving to the Lord first is an act of faith that recognizes God as your provider. Rather than leaning on your own strength, you're depending on God to provide not only for you but also for those you care most about. And in case you didn't know it, God is a much better provider than you are—because He has access to many more resources than you do. So honor Him with your first and best, and He will do the rest.

Now, I know the question on your mind right now: *How much should I give?* That's between you and God. That's a conversation you need to have with Jesus, then allow Him to lead you to whatever is best and appropriate in your situation.

I will give you my opinion: throughout Scripture, the tithe is the starting place for giving to God. Throughout all of God's Word, the people who were faithful to God started by giving 10 percent of their income—whether that was animals from the flock, produce from the fields, cash money, or whatever. They gave 10 percent of their income as a tithe, and several times in both the Old and New Testaments we see God's people going above and beyond the tithe by giving "offerings."

I love the illustration Randy Alcorn uses in his book *The Treasure Principle*. He says the tithe is like training wheels. Training wheels help us learn how to ride a bike, but once we learn, we get to take them off and enjoy the ride. The tithe is similar. It helps us learn the faith principle of trusting God with the first and best of what He gave us; but once we learn the freedom that comes through generosity, we'll see ourselves grow far beyond a tithe.[7]

For example, when my wife and I first got married, we structured our finances so that we gave the first 10 percent to the Lord. I have to be honest, but in those early days it was scary. We were really nervous. But now, decades later, having watched God provide supernaturally in ways we never could have imagined, we're able to enjoy living well beyond the tithe. The fear is gone, and now we're excited about what God will do as we honor Him.

What you give is between you and God. But whatever you decide, be sure to give to God first. That's key for reducing the stressors in your life connected to money.

Save for the Future

I recently heard a statistic from the Federal Reserve that shocked me: as of 2020, 39 percent of Americans didn't have enough money on hand to cover a $400 emergency. That's four out of every ten people! Four out of every ten households.[8]

Talk about a stressor! If you want to remove a big portion of the stress connected to your finances, one very practical step you can take is to start saving for the future. In fact, if generously giving to the Lord is the first step you take, the second step should be wisely preparing for the future by placing a portion of that income into your savings.

Look at what Proverbs says:

> The wise have wealth and luxury,
> but fools spend whatever they get. (21:20 NLT)

Again, this isn't me talking to you. This is just me holding up the mirror of Scripture. And that mirror shows that if you're not saving for the future, you're acting foolishly. You're inviting stress into your life.

Once again, I'm sure you're wondering, *How much should I save?* And once again, that's a decision you need to make in conversation with God. Every person and every household is unique.

Personally, my family has committed to saving a minimum of 10 percent of our income for the future. Whenever we get a paycheck, we have things set up so that our first payment is to God—we're serious about seeking His kingdom first. Then, even before we have access to that money, at least 10 percent of it is transferred to our savings accounts, which include our retirement account.

Whatever number you land on, you must understand that living within your means is more than simply not spending more than you make. From a biblical perspective, living wisely includes saving for the future.

Budget to Live

Here's another shocking statistic I uncovered while researching for this chapter: according to a recent survey, 65 percent of Americans had no idea how much they spent last month. That's three out of every five people. It's not surprising, then, that the same survey showed 31 percent of Americans regretted how much they spent in the previous month.[9]

To honor God with your finances, you need to give to Him first, save for the future second, and then set up and follow a plan to manage your finances that you can actually keep track of. In other words, you need a budget.

Here's another bit of wisdom from Proverbs:

> The plans of the diligent lead surely to advantage,
> But everyone who is hasty comes surely to poverty.
> (21:5 NASB1995)

Wisdom demands that we manage our money with an intentional purpose—and promises that when we do, we'll be in a favorable financial position.

In other words, the Bible says if you set a budget and live by it, you'll be better off. It's not rocket science!

However, "Everyone who is hasty comes surely to poverty." The word translated "hasty" in that verse is the Hebrew term for doing something on the spur of the moment. So, if you just spend your money on whatever happens to be in front of you in the moment—"Hey, that looks really fun. Let's get two!"—the Bible says you're going to come to poverty. You're not going to have enough resources to cover your needs.

And you know what poverty brings to your life? Stress. Lots and lots of stress.

Earlier I mentioned three layers of the bull's-eye for honoring God with your finances. Let's revisit that idea, but let's add some numbers to it as a goal. Specifically, here's a double-click on the bull's-eye you can use to honor God with your money:

- Give 10 percent of your resources to the Lord.
- Save 10 percent of your resources for the future.
- Budget to live on the remaining 80 percent.

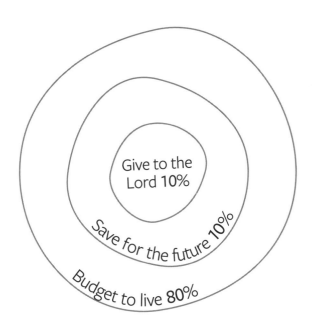

Now, that's just a suggestion. You need to fill in the numbers based on your unique situation and understanding of Scripture. But whatever numbers you come up with, it's critical that you have a target you're aiming at with your finances and a plan for honoring God with your money.

Not only that, but you also need to spend a little time checking your aim. Meaning, are you hitting the target you set? If you plan to give God 10 percent, you need to take a look at the end of each month or the end of each year and see if that actually happened. That's what it means to honor God with your money.

When Kristie and I first got married, we wanted to be good stewards and established this 10/10/80 target for our family. I was working part-time and attending college, and Kristie was a nanny for a family. We were so poor I couldn't afford textbooks. I just took good notes and hit up the library to borrow books. Our plan was to wait until after college to have kids, but God had other plans. Three months after we got married, my wife got pregnant. Panic set in! I was so worried about how I was going to provide. Still, Kristie and I talked and prayed and pressed on with our target.

During the pregnancy, Kristie had some heart irregularities that required her to be on a heart monitor for a twenty-four-hour test. When we got the bill, panic set in again. It was for $672. That was more than we had in the bank and about half of what we were making each month. I'll never forget that feeling of failure as a new husband and father-to-be.

I remember driving home one day, burdened about this situation. All at once, the Holy Spirit whispered in my ear, "The Lord is my Shepherd, I shall not want." I sensed an unexplainable peace. I got home and Kristie handed me the mail with a shocked look on her face. In the mail was a tax refund check for $675 dollars. God not only provided for our needs, but He also gave us some extra money to go to McDonald's to celebrate!

Over and over again in our family, we've learned that when we honor God with our finances, we can trust Him to satisfy all our needs. And the reality is, He does so above and beyond!

How to Trust God to Satisfy Your Needs

Let's get back to Jesus. The key principle we've been working through is that when we honor God with our finances, we can trust Him to satisfy all our needs.

Now, that statement has two parts. We've already talked about the first one. We've seen that to remove stress when it comes to money, we have to honor God by properly handling whatever He gives us. That means giving back to God, saving for the future, and budgeting to live.

What about the second part? How do we trust that God will satisfy our needs? Well, Jesus showed us several reasons why we can trust the Father when it comes to money.

First, we can trust God because of His relationship with us. There are two times in Matthew 6 that Jesus emphasizes God's role as our "heavenly Father." Focus for a moment on that term *Father*. If you're a parent, have you ever gone into a week thinking, *Maybe I won't meet my children's needs for the next few days?* Of course not! Parents love their children, which means they're willing to sacrifice anything in order to provide for them.

Now look at what Jesus said later in His Sermon on the Mount: "If you then, being evil, know how to give good gifts to your children, how much more will your Father who is in heaven give what is good to those who ask Him!" (Matt. 7:11 NASB 1995).

That points to another truth: not only is God our Father; He's our *heavenly* Father. This term emphasizes the bigness of God. His sovereignty.

Let me ask you a question: What are you stressed out about right now? What's keeping you up at night? What are the problems or difficulties or struggles that right now seem way more than your resources can match? Can you see that problem in your mind? If so, I want you to know that God is bigger. Speaking plainly, there's no problem you could ever face that's bigger than God. There's nothing in the universe bigger than Him! Therefore, you can trust Him to satisfy your needs.

The second reason you can trust God to satisfy your needs is because of His abundance for you. We've already seen how Jesus desires "abundant life" for His followers, but I like how the apostle Paul describes that abundance. He writes, "And my God will supply all your needs according to His riches in glory in Christ Jesus" (Phil. 4:19).

Listen, God has enough to bless you. For one thing, God doesn't supply for *your needs* based on *your resources*. Thank goodness! He supplies for you based on His resources. Not only that, but God also doesn't take care of your needs out of the crumbs that fall from His table. No, He satisfies your needs "according to His riches in glory."

You can trust God to satisfy your needs because He has more than enough.

Lastly, you can trust God because of His value for you. In His sermon, Jesus described many ways in which God takes care of elements from the natural world. He watches over the birds of the sky. He clothes the flowers and the grasses in splendor.

Then Jesus asked a powerful question: "Are you not much more important than they?" (Matt. 6:26). Yes, you're much more valuable. You're the crown of God's creation. And I don't mean "you" in a general sense, like humanity. I mean *you*, the person reading this book. You, the person looking to be filled with God's peace. You're incredibly valuable to God.

How do I know that? Because Scripture also says, "But God demonstrates His own love toward us, in that while we were still sinners, Christ died for us" (Rom. 5:8). You're so important to God that He shed His own blood for you—so that you could know Him and enjoy a relationship with Him, for all eternity.

Notice again that Jesus said, "Your heavenly Father knows that you need all these things" (Matt. 6:32). God not only values you, but He also knows you intimately. He knows everything you need. Out of His love and abundance, He desires to satisfy those needs.

Therefore, don't worry. Don't let the stressors connected to money drive you to feel stressed.

Instead, choose to trust God. As we conclude this chapter, I want you to read this truth out loud and let it lead you toward peace:

I am to trust God with everything in my life by honoring Him with what He has given to me, and He promises to always satisfy me with enough.

5

Dealing with People

How Do I Find God's Peace in My Relationships?

On July 9, 2020, Jimmy and Joanie Goodman celebrated their wedding anniversary right in the middle of the COVID-19 pandemic. Being under quarantine was disappointing because they weren't able to share the occasion with their friends and family. But the Goodmans understood most people were facing the same dilemma with other important moments—graduations, weddings, holidays, and even funerals were all locked down.

Still, the Goodmans' special occasion wasn't like what most other people were experiencing. Why? Because it was their seventieth wedding anniversary!

As you might expect from a couple with such a long history, Jimmy and Joanie were unfazed by the trouble gripping the world outside their doors. "We're just happy to be here and do whatever we can because we're locked up," Joanie said. "What are you gonna do? You make the best of it."[1]

The Goodmans' love story began all the way back in the 1940s. They met when Joanie was sixteen and Jimmy was twenty. "He took me out to dinner for my birthday and we've been together ever since," said Joanie.[2] Even when she went to college, she knew Jimmy was waiting for her. "He was already out of college, and we got pinned," she said. "That's what they used to do. You'd wear a fraternity pin that meant you were going to be engaged."[3]

Throughout their seventy years of marriage, Jimmy and Joanie led the kind of life that my kids might describe as #relationshipgoals. They ran a business together for thirty years. They saw the world. They built a home. At the time of their seventieth anniversary, they had three children, eight grandchildren, and nine great-grandchildren.

When asked how they had maintained such a strong relationship for so long, Jimmy offered just three words: "Love and respect."

Of course, it wasn't all ups. There were some downs sprinkled in here and there. According to Joanie, one of the most difficult trials was Jimmy's love of poker. He spent a lot of time traveling for work, but then he'd want to play poker with his buddies during the weekend. "It wasn't like he wanted to play poker from 7:00 p.m. to 9:00 p.m.," Joanie said. "It was like he wanted to play poker from 7:00 p.m. until 3:00 a.m., and that was heavy duty."[4] Admittedly, she had her own issues, including a love of shopping, "but that didn't go away either."

Amazingly, according to Joanie, "that was the only stress. Otherwise, we got along beautifully."[5]

As a married man, I'm sure I'm not the only person who read the Goodmans' story and said, "What? That was the only stress?!" In fact, most of us would say the Goodmans are the exception that proves the rule—because marriage is often stressful.

And not just marriage. At Hope Church, we say all the time that "following Jesus is all about relationships," which is true. But we could easily add another statement to that: "and relationships can be stressful."

The statistics back up that claim. Once again, looking at recent surveys from the American Psychological Association, 44 percent of Americans identified relationships as either a "very significant" or "somewhat significant" source of stress in their lives. And it's not just romantic relationships. Forty-seven percent of Americans said family responsibilities were a high source of stress. Plus, parents reported higher average stress levels than nonparents—and parents were more likely than nonparents to say their stress levels increased during the past year.[6]

So, yes, relationships can be a major source of stress in our lives—but they don't have to be.

As a reminder, stressors are the circumstances in our lives that create pressure, tension, and strain. When stressors cause us to look toward God, they can result in God's peace. When we try to solve stressors by looking to our own resources, however, they lead to stress.

Here's the question for this chapter, then: How do we remove as many stressors as possible from our relationships? Beyond that, how do we handle the remaining stressors in a way that allows us to receive God's peace rather than be crushed by stress?

I want to answer those questions by exploring two key realities when it comes to relationships.

There Are Times in Relationships When We Need to Change

The first principle when it comes to removing stressors from our relationships is coming to the understanding that we're often the cause of those stressors. Meaning, a lot of the stress we experience in our relationships comes not from them but from us. From you and me.

If you feel a little let down right now, you're not alone. Whenever I preach about relationships at our church, I see the way people perk up. They straighten in their seats. They give me their full attention. And I know exactly what they're thinking as they contemplate that person or persons in their lives—sometimes sitting right next to them. *Please tell me how to fix them.*

Well, you can't fix them. Whoever comes to mind right now as part of a relationship causing stress in your life, please know there's nothing you can do to change that person or those people. But you can change yourself. In fact, the stress you're experiencing from that relationship or those relationships just might be an indicator that something about you needs to change.

A few books have meant so much to me over the course of my life that I read them every year. One of those is a little paperback called *The Calvary Road*, written by a brilliant man named Roy Hession. This book is mainly about relationships within the body of Christ, and it's filled with practical wisdom.

Here's what Hession writes about the theme of relational conflict or relational stress:

> We shall have to see that the thing in us that reacts so sharply to another's selfishness and pride is simply our own selfishness and pride, which we are unwilling to sacrifice. We shall have to accept another's ways and doings as God's will for us and meekly bend the neck to all of God's providences. That does not mean we must accept another's selfishness as God's will for them—far from it—but only as God's will for us.[7]

What Hession means is that God often allows difficult people into our lives for a reason. God wants to do things in us—shape us and grow us in certain ways—that can be accomplished only through others. Perhaps especially those "others" who make us feel stressed.

So, if we're really going to deal with this issue of removing stress from our relationships, we must begin by looking on the inside and asking, *What does God want to do in me?*

That's the theme of the Scripture passage I want to focus on for this chapter, which is from the book of Ephesians:

> Therefore, ridding yourselves of falsehood, speak truth each one of you with his neighbor, because we are parts of one another. Be angry, and yet do not sin; do not let the sun go down on your anger, and do not give the devil an opportunity. The one who steals must no longer steal; but rather he must labor, producing with his own hands what is good, so that he will have something to share with the one who has need. Let no unwholesome word come out of your mouth, but if there is any good word for edification according to the need of the

moment, say that, so that it will give grace to those who hear. Do not grieve the Holy Spirit of God, by whom you were sealed for the day of redemption. All bitterness, wrath, anger, clamor, and slander must be removed from you, along with all malice. Be kind to one another, compassionate, forgiving each other, just as God in Christ also has forgiven you. (4:25–32)

To give you a little background, Paul was writing to a young church in Ephesus. When he wrote the letter we know as Ephesians, that church had been in existence for only six years, which meant all the people in the church had been Jesus followers for a maximum of six years. Many in the congregation had been following Christ for only weeks or months. They were immature in their faith.

The "therefore" present at the start of Ephesians 4 refers to verses 17–24, in which Paul makes the point that Jesus followers should "no longer walk just as the Gentiles also walk, in the futility of their minds" (v. 17). *Gentiles* of course was a slang term for unbelievers. Paul wanted this young congregation to see that following Jesus means walking differently from the rest of the world, including in our relationships.

Speaking of young Christians, I was twenty-three years old when I pastored my first church. I can tell you that God used a lot of relationships during my experience there to grow me in many ways. For example, my first week on the job, the leaders of the church gathered together and I met with them. At that point in my life, I was really young, really energetic, and really naïve. I was so full of vision and passion for all the things I knew God was about to do in our community.

A couple of other guys and I were walking down the hall toward that first meeting when they stopped me for a minute. They said, "Pastor, we just want you to be aware that so-and-so will be in this meeting." They were talking about an older gentleman who was one of the leaders in the church.

I said, "That's great! I've got some exciting things to share about what God's doing on my heart, and I—"

They stopped me again and said, "No, you don't understand. He's going to be in this meeting, and he's going to be against everything you say."

That didn't make sense to me. "He doesn't even know what I'm going to say yet!"

They said, "Doesn't matter. He's against everything that everybody says."

I had to ask, "How long has this guy been in our church?"

"About twenty-five years."

Looking back, the thing that still bothers me most about that whole situation is that it didn't bother them. They were used to that kind of behavior. They thought it was normal.

They weren't the only ones. I tell that story because it's common within the body of Christ today for people to label themselves as Jesus followers, yet continue living the same old lives they've always lived. I'm not saying everyone should go from Saul to Paul—from murdering Christians to preaching the gospel—in a matter of days. Sometimes that happens; often it doesn't.

What I'm saying is this: when Jesus Christ comes to live inside us, He changes the way we live. Christ living in us and through us should transform us from the inside out. And one of the primary ways we experience that change is in our relationships—the presence of Jesus should radically change how we relate to other people.

With all that in mind, I want to give you five questions you can ask if you're experiencing stress in your relationships. Remember, if a particular relationship is bringing stressors into your life, the first place you need to look is inside. Are there areas you need to change? Is God doing something in you through this relationship? These five questions will give you a starting point to help you take that look inside.

Am I Being Honest in This Relationship?

Paul jumps right into this topic in verse 25 by addressing an issue at the core of healthy relationships: honesty. Look at what he says: "Therefore, ridding yourselves of falsehood, speak truth each one of you with his neighbor, because we are parts of one another."

The word translated "falsehood" is a general term for lying or speaking dishonestly. It includes both lying through what we say and lying through what we don't say. Paul wants us to get rid of all of it. "Ridding yourselves of falsehood."

Then Paul gives another imperative. Another command: "Speak truth each one of you." In the original language, the word translated "speak" is in the present-active tense, which means it's ongoing. We could translate it as "keep on speaking truth." Keep on being honest.

Here's another one of those simple questions: Are you honest in your relationships? More to the point, are any relationships in your life stressors because you're avoiding honesty—or because you're being outright dishonest?

Maybe you say, *What does that even look like, Vance? What does it mean to be honest in my relationships?*

Well, here's a quick example. Elements in every relationship can be stressful, and that's especially true in marriage.

After thirty years of marriage, Kristie and I have come to a pretty good understanding of what each of us does that stresses the other person out.

For example, for me, it's being late. I hate being late. In fact, I'm one of those people who considers "on time" to mean arriving fifteen minutes early. My wife wasn't built that way. She prefers the "how" to the "when." She would rather get someplace looking the way she prefers and feeling prepared, rather than worrying about the exact time she was supposed to get there. On top of that, probably the biggest thing that stresses her out in our relationship is when I get stressed out about being late. She really doesn't like it when I start trying to herd her out the door like a sheepdog. "It's 10:45, honey. Do you have your purse? Shouldn't your shoes be on by now?"

So this issue of punctuality is a potential stressor in our relationship. And what it means to be honest in our relationship is for each of us to communicate truthfully, but with love, about what we're feeling and what we would like to happen.

I might say, "Kristie, this meeting is an important one for me, and I would really like for us to be on time." She might say, "Vance, you know the restaurant isn't going to cancel our reservation if we get there a few minutes late, so I'd like to get ready in peace." Those would apply to specific situations, but even more generally, the more we communicate honestly about what causes us to feel stress, the more we learn about each other and the more we're able to serve each other in our relationship.

What's the alternative? To clam up. To refuse to say anything because we don't want conflict. That might seem like a good idea in the short term, but it's not honest. It's not being real with each other, and it'll cause a lot of difficulty in the long term. A lot of stress.

Am I Harboring Anger about the Past?

Failing to be honest within our relationships produces not only stress but also anger. And carrying around anger in our hearts isn't helpful or healthy. We feel that anger whenever we see that other person, which, again, causes us to feel stressed; it's a vicious cycle. So, the second question to ask when you encounter stress in a relationship is whether you're holding on to anger within that relationship because of something that happened in the past.

Back to our Scripture passage, Paul writes, "Be angry, and yet do not sin; do not let the sun go down on your anger, and do not give the devil an opportunity" (vv. 26–27).

That almost sounds schizophrenic, doesn't it? It seems as if Paul is saying both *be angry* and *don't be angry*. But we need to understand he used two separate words for anger in the original language. The first word ("be angry, and yet do not sin") is a generic word for anger or becoming provoked. That kind of anger could be good or bad, since anger in and of itself is not a bad thing; you can be righteously angry. The second term ("do not let the sun go down on your anger") is different. It describes a seething exasperation or a deep-seated resentment over something that has been done to someone. It means the type of anger that doesn't let go but just festers inside. That kind of anger is never good or healthy or helpful.

This second type of anger is what I'm talking about when I ask whether you're feeling stress in a relationship because you're harboring anger from something that happened in the past. Are you holding on to an anger that festers and seethes inside you?

If so, it's a problem. When you live with that kind of anger trickling in and through a relationship—especially an important relationship—you begin to see the other person through an angry lens. Your perception of everything that person says or does is colored by the anger you've allowed to fester inside you. Therefore, interacting with that person produces anxiety and stress.

Here's a question: Is there someone in your life who, even the sight of them, causes you to feel anxious or stressed out? If so, you need to understand that's not about them—that's about you. You're hanging on to something from the past that needs to be dealt with through Christ, and then you need to let it go.

When you refuse to let it go, Paul says you "give the devil an opportunity." You not only allow stress in your life but also give your enemy a foothold to cause more and more destruction. You make room for the devil in your life, and that's always a bad idea.

Roy Hession has another quote about this topic that, for me, is both wise and practical. He writes, "God wants me to see that it was not the thing the person did that matters, but my reaction to it."[8]

Are you holding on to anger from the past? Are you allowing that anger to produce stress in your relationships? If so, that's an area you need to change. And by changing you can significantly reduce the number of stressors you have to deal with each day.

Am I Focused on What I Can Get or What I Can Give?

This third question is a tough one. It's one of those questions that requires some serious introspection, but it's necessary if we want to remove stressors and stress from our relationships. When you encounter a relationship that causes stress, take some time to evaluate whether you're focused on what you can get from that relationship or what you can give to it.

In other words, am I stressed out in my relationship because I have the wrong focus?

Paul has this to say: "The one who steals must no longer steal; but rather he must labor, producing with his own hands what is good, so that he will have something to share with the one who has need" (v. 28).

> When you encounter a relationship that causes stress, take some time to evaluate whether you're focused on what you can get from that relationship or what you can give to it.

You might think, *What in the world does that have to do with relationships?* Well, a lot actually. The word translated "share" at the end of that verse is a very relational term in the original language. It's not the regular word for sharing that's used throughout the New Testament—such as sharing some loaves and fishes. This particular term is actually a compound word that could literally be translated "give with." The idea is "giving with" the people in my life or sharing life with those around me.

Interestingly and importantly, this whole concept of sharing, or giving with, is contrasted with stealing. If you were to talk with our neighbors, they might tell you our family has an obsession with Amazon. I can't confirm or deny whether that's true, but we do get packages delivered to our house multiple times every week—sometimes every day. Groceries, household items, generic supplies, gifts for the grandkids, and more.

Because we get so many deliveries, Kristie and I have the Ring app on our phones. One day I got an alert through that app that warned about porch pirates—people who steal packages from other people's homes. This was all new to me, and I was astounded that folks could be so brazen in their thievery that they would just walk up to someone's house, grab a package, and walk away.

Then I did some research. Did you know almost 40 percent of Americans have had packages stolen from their homes in the past year?[9] That's crazy! Not only that, but researchers also estimate that 1.7 million packages are stolen or lost *every single day* in the United States. Every day![10] I've paid a lot closer attention to that Ring app on my phone ever since.

I have a hard time even imagining the mindset of a thief. We just don't see the world in the same way. A thief must look around and see possessions not as things that belong to other people but as objects that *could* belong to them—if only they have the skill and boldness to grab them. Thieves believe they're entitled to what belongs to somebody else.

What Paul is saying in this verse is that we often have a similar mindset when it comes to our relationships. We treat people as if they exist to meet our needs. We see relationships—or maybe only certain relationships—primarily as opportunities to get something.

Here's what this looks like on a practical level. If you view a relationship as a means of getting something, then you will attach a lot of expectations to that relationship. You'll think, whether consciously or unconsciously, *I like hanging out with John because he always makes me laugh.* Or *Sheila is a great lunch date because she always pays.* Or even, *My mom is always happy to watch my kids when I need a break.* Do you see the problem there? We approach these relationships with a sense of entitlement and expectation. But then what happens when the other person doesn't meet those expectations? What happens when they don't give us what we expect them to give? We feel stressed.

If that's true for you right now—if you're feeling stress in a relationship because the other person isn't fulfilling the responsibility you've assigned to them—you need to come back to Paul's instruction to share. To "give with." Maybe God doesn't have that person in your life because of what they can do for you; maybe God brought them to you because of what He desires to do for them through you.

When you understand that reality, you'll find a lot of stressors are suddenly removed from your relationships.

Am I Looking for Opportunities to Speak Grace?

Quick test: What would you say is the most powerful force in the universe? How you answer that question probably says a lot about you.

If you're a scientist, for example, you might say the most powerful force in the universe is the strong nuclear force, which binds subatomic particles together. Apparently this force is six thousand trillion trillion trillion times stronger than gravity![11] If you're a philosopher, you might say love is the strongest force in the universe. (And you would have a point, since the Bible says God is love.) Or, if you're a financial person, you might agree with Albert Einstein's idea that the most powerful force in the universe is compounding interest.

Personally, I have no idea what the most powerful force in the universe is. But I do know this: when it comes to relationships, few things are more powerful than words. That's why the author of Proverbs writes, "Death and life are in the power of the tongue" (18:21).

Here's what Paul writes about the power and importance of words in our relationships: "Let no unwholesome word come out of your mouth, but if there is any good word for edification according to the need of the moment, say that, so that it will give grace to those who hear" (Eph. 4:29).

Paul communicates three things in that verse, and the first is that what we say matters. Obviously, that means we should reject any kind of "unwholesome word." We should never engage in speech that is rotten, repulsive, or designed to tear someone down. Why? Because death and life are in the power of the tongue. Words are powerful.

Just as importantly, Paul contrasts "unwholesome words" with "edification," which is the process of building someone up. And this is important: Paul doesn't say we should avoid destructive words and throw out some constructive words every now and then. No, he writes, "If there is *any* good word for edification according to the need of the moment, say that" (emphasis added).

Paul instructs you and me to look for every opportunity we can find to speak grace into the lives of others. Or, to say it another way, in my relationships, everything I say should be intended to build up the person I am speaking to. Why? Because words matter. What we say matters.

The second thing Paul communicates in verse 29 is that *when* we say what we say is also important. The timing of our words matters. Look again at verse 29: "Let no unwholesome word come out of your mouth, but if there is any good word for edification *according to the need of the moment*, say that, so that it will give grace to those who hear" (emphasis added).

Here's the reality: it's possible to say the right thing at the wrong moment. If we're not intentional about offering grace through the timing of our words, we can create stress in our relationships.

Finally, the third thing Paul communicates in verse 29 is that *how* we say what we say when we say it is very important. The tone of our words matters. The end of verse 29 says, "So that it will give grace to those who hear."

Here's another reality: it's possible to say the right thing at the right time but say it in the wrong way—especially if we're stressed out! Paul says the way we talk to others should be designed to give grace. Or, to phrase this differently, the way we say something can determine whether the one we're speaking to accepts what we say.

Paul gives a similar piece of advice in Colossians 4:6 when he writes, "Let your speech always be with grace, as though seasoned with salt, so that you will know how you should respond to each person" (NASB1995).

I know those three elements of communication may seem complicated, but they really boil down to a pretty simple idea: the way we communicate can bring either life or death to our relationships. How do we know when our communication is bringing death? When it creates stress. In such situations, we need to ask ourselves if *what* we say is causing stress, if *when* we say it is causing stress, or if *how* we say it is causing stress. And the solution to any of those problems is to use every opportunity we can find to speak grace into the lives of others.

Am I Dealing with This Relationship in My Own Strength?

The fifth and final question we can use to evaluate stressful relationships in our lives comes from Paul's words in Ephesians 4:31–32: "All bitterness, wrath, anger, clamor, and slander must be removed from you, along with all malice. Be kind to one another, compassionate, forgiving each other, just as God in Christ also has forgiven you."

Here's the question to ask yourself: Am I dealing with this relationship in my own strength, or am I allowing Christ to live through me?

This is another of those places in Scripture where we have two stark options. On the one hand, we can try to "manage" our relationships through our own abilities. We can relate to others through our own resources and strengths and wits and all that. As you've already guessed, this is a bad idea. Why? Because we don't have very many resources! No matter how patient or grace-filled we might be, we eventually wear out and wear thin—especially in our dealings with people. And the result is all the bad things Paul mentioned: bitterness, wrath, anger, clamor, slander, malice, and so on.

Thankfully, Paul gives us another list. This is the alternative to managing relationships through our own resources: "Be kind to one another, compassionate, forgiving each other."

How do we accomplish these things? Look at the end of the verse: "just as God in Christ also has forgiven you," meaning we don't accomplish those things in our relationships. Jesus does.

We don't have the capacity to be kind in our relationships. Not all the time. There will come a moment when our strength runs out, we snap, and then we experience stress. But Jesus has the capacity for infinite kindness. In the same way, we don't have the capacity to be compassionate in all our relationships—to understand others and empathize. But Jesus does. Always. And we don't have the capacity to forgive those who wrong us. But Jesus does, just like He forgave us.

Here's the reality: you don't have the strength to remove bitterness and wrath and slander and all those unhelpful things. That's one reason your relationships are filled with stress. The solution, then, is to allow Jesus to live His life in and through you in your relationships with others. Doing so will not only improve your relationships but also remove quite a few stressors from your life and allow you to experience God's peace more fully.

I'll conclude this section with one more quote from Roy Hession: "Every humiliation, everyone who tries and vexes us, is God's way of breaking us so that there is yet a deeper channel in us for the life of Christ."[12]

There Are Times When a Relationship Needs to Change

If you're part of a relationship that is producing stressors or causing stress in your life, then something needs to change. And let me emphasize once again that it's most likely you who needs to change. When stress is in your relationships, you need to start by examining yourself and asking the five questions we just went through to determine whether and where something needs to be adjusted in your life.

Let me say this: the first thing you need to do when dealing with stressful relationships is examine your own heart. Better yet, get honest before God and ask His Spirit to examine your heart and point out any areas that need to change. And I'd also recommend you seek out godly counsel from people you trust who can speak truth to you.

That's the first step. But there's also a second step. Because sometimes you won't be the problem. That's why Paul says, "If possible, so far as it depends on you, be at peace with all people" (Rom. 12:18). Sometimes it doesn't depend on you. Sometimes the relationship itself needs to change. Something must be adjusted to remove those stressors or prevent stress from squeezing your life.

So, in the final pages of this chapter, I want to present three steps you can take to change a relationship that's causing stress.

Step Up

The first step you should take is what I call "step up." That means confronting the relationship—confronting the person or persons who are the source of stress.

If the word *confront* sets your teeth on edge, I understand. I don't like conflict either. I don't like confrontation. The good news is, I'm not talking about confronting someone in the way our culture usually understands that word. I'm not talking about a reality TV confrontation, with yelling and accusations and throwing things across the room.

No, I'm talking about a biblical confrontation, which means it needs to be rooted in the desire for peace. Again, Scripture says, "If possible, so far as it depends on you, be at peace with all people" (Rom. 12:18). That means as Jesus followers, you and I are called to do everything in our power to pursue peace with other people—even during moments of confrontation.

Now you're asking, *How do I confront someone in a way that is rooted in peace?* Thankfully, Jesus gave us the answer to that question in Matthew 18:

> Now if your brother sins, go and show him his fault in private; if he listens to you, you have gained your brother. But if he does not listen to you, take one or two more with you, so that on the testimony of two or three witnesses every matter may be confirmed. And if he refuses to listen to them, tell it to the church; and if he refuses to listen even to the church, he is to be to you as a Gentile and a tax collector. (vv. 15–17)

What Jesus described is a fourfold process for reconciliation within relationships. First, that means having a private conversation with the other person or people. And this is where honesty once again comes into play. It means going to the other person and saying, "There's something off in our relationship. Something is broken, and its causing stress in my life. So, I'd like to sit down with you and see if we can figure this out together."

The key is that this is a private conversation. This isn't something you post on social media. This isn't one of those moments where you go to the people around you and say, "I need to tell you what so-and-so is doing so you can pray about it with me." No, Jesus said to start with a private conversation. At this point in the relationship, you want to assume the best, and are simply communicating to clarify.

And if that conversation is successful—if it leads to reconciliation—the Bible says that's a win. "You have gained your brother."

If that conversation doesn't resolve things, Jesus told us what to do next: "Take one or two more with you, so that on the testimony of two or three witnesses every matter may be confirmed." Now, Jesus wasn't saying you should find one or two people who are on your side so you can put the full-court press on the person you're confronting. No!

Instead, if you and the other person have talked through the situation together, yet you're still on different sides about the problem, you need some objective counsel. You need one or two people outside the situation who can listen to both of you and determine what might be off track. The goal is to find those who can bring clarity to the reconciliation process.

If that doesn't work, Jesus said, "Tell it to the church." Not the whole church! Jesus wasn't saying you should make accusations on the church Facebook page. Instead, He was talking about involving spiritual leadership. Talk to someone with spiritual authority over both you and the other person—a pastor or a small group leader. And again, the goal is to find someone objective who can bring clarity and lead you both toward resolution.

Jesus's final instruction sounds strange to modern ears: "If he refuses to listen even to the church, he is to be to you as a Gentile and a tax collector" (v. 17). In Jesus's day, *Gentile* and *tax collector* were terms that referred to unbelievers. People who had not encountered God.

What was Jesus saying? Simply this: if you go through those first three actions and you're still unable to find reconciliation with the other party, you need to pray for them as if they don't even know the Lord. You need to shift your focus from trying to restore the relationship to praying they can be restored in their fellowship with God.

One thing before we move on: this process isn't intended to work only between Christians. It'll work for any relational conflict—between neighbors, coworkers, family members, and more. If you go to any conflict-resolution speaker, they'll teach you a version of this process. Even if they don't acknowledge that the process comes from Jesus or has its source in the Bible, this is what they'll use.

Because it works.

Step Back

The first step in changing a stressful relationship is to step up and confront the situation. The second step is what I call "step back," which means establishing boundaries for the relationship.

Now, let me say something before we move forward. If the relationship in question involves someone in your immediate family—a spouse, a child, a sibling, or a parent—and if you've exhausted all the options up to this point, I don't recommend moving forward with step two or step three (below). Instead, I suggest you sit down with a spiritual leader and seek counsel in that relationship. Perhaps even to the level of professional counsel.

I need to throw in one disclaimer. If you're living in an abusive situation, it isn't God's desire or design for you to remain in that situation. You should seek immediate help to remove yourself from that relationship and find biblical counsel to guide you through your healing and decision-making process. A true gospel-centered church will be ready to stand with you, and God's grace will see you through!

Having said this, there will be times in your general relationships with neighbors, coworkers, friends, and so on when you need to establish boundaries in order to prevent stressors from piling up. And by boundaries, I mean you take the lead in that relationship. You determine how often you spend time with the other person and where the relationship goes.

What does that look like? Well, it might start with the simple decision to say no. "No, I can't get together for lunch tomorrow." "No, I'm not going to answer the phone every time you call." "No, I don't want to participate in that activity because it's not good for me."

Setting boundaries also includes actively declaring what you are and aren't comfortable with—and then being firm in keeping those boundaries. "I will do this with you, but I won't do that." "We can get together this many times in a month but not more." "These are the places I'll go with you, and these are the places I won't go."

Once again, I advise you to seek counsel as you establish these boundaries. Why? Because emotional involvement often leads to poor decisions. Speaking personally, I believe I'm someone who gives good counsel and generally makes good decisions. But when I'm emotionally invested in a relationship, my judgment gets blurred and I need to seek the advice of others.

However you make it happen, the key is that you must set boundaries on the amount of influence stressful relationships have in your life.

Step Away

The final step for changing a stressful relationship is to "step away." That means removing the relationship from your life, whether for a set period of time or indefinitely.

If that sounds harsh, I know. It's the final option for a reason. But if you have a tooth that's rotten to the core and causing you great pain, there comes a time when the only solution is to have it removed. If your appendix is inflamed and about to burst, trying to manage it and smooth things over will only put you in greater danger. It has to go.

So, if there's a relationship that's producing stress and you have confronted it and invested yourself in trying to set boundaries—if all that has failed, and if the relationship is still a source of stress, then the wise thing to do is let it go.

Having said that, remember this: you should never give up on God's ability to change a person. Removing a relationship from your life doesn't mean writing that person off completely. It doesn't mean erasing them from your memory or your thoughts—or especially your prayers.

Instead, leave room for God to do a work of transformation in the other person's life. And when that happens, be the first one to come running toward them with an offer of reconciliation.

Here's the bottom line: relationships can be stressful. Relationships are often a huge source of stressors. When you find yourself in that situation, the first thing you should consider is whether you need to change within that relationship. Where is God calling you to grow and develop because of that relationship? When you identify that need and allow God to transform you, you will uncover a deeper level of His peace.

There will also be times when the relationship needs to change—when you need to step up by confronting that relationship, step back by establishing some boundaries, or step away from that relationship for a season. And always remember that going through the process of dealing with stress in a relationship isn't so you can have an easier life or avoid being bothered. Rather, it's so you can be filled to an even greater level with *the peace of God.*

6

Choices, Choices

How Do I Find God's Peace in My Decision-Making?

I'll never forget the day I watched a man write a million-dollar check. The mixture of relief, fear, and responsibility I felt as I put that check in my pocket is something I haven't experienced since and I don't think I care to experience again.

To give you a little background on that moment, our church has gone through the wringer on several occasions in terms of finding a place to meet. I mentioned that in the introduction, but things really came to a head around 2008. We'd been growing for years at that point, and we were so far over capacity in our meeting space that we simply had to make a change.

Our first thought was to find another property to lease, but that proved impossible. In fact, over the course of a few weeks, my team and I looked at ninety-six rental properties we thought had potential—and every single one turned us down. None of them would rent to a house of worship.

So we had no choice but to build a place of our own.

Things started out well—at least as well as we could have hoped for in the middle of a recession. No bank would work with us, but we were able to raise a lot of the necessary funds by selling bonds. We had a property. We had plans and schematics. The construction crews started digging.

And that's when everything went off the rails. Our bond company got sued for a product it had sold ten years prior and went out of business. We had a building that was 70 percent finished but had no occupancy permit, so we couldn't use it. We had no lending institution, so we couldn't finish the building. And we had no money in the bank, so we couldn't rent anything else as a permanent solution.

We were stuck.

Finally, I called one of our church members who was a person of means. I told him, "I need a million dollars yesterday. Do you know anyone in the city who might lend that kind of money to the church?" I was really hoping he could leverage his influence with a bank or some other institution.

He said, "No, I don't know anybody. But you're talking to a guy who can do it."

Later the same day, I sat down in his office while his accountant wrote that check. Then I spent the whole drive to the bank praising and thanking God. That wasn't the end of our problems—God still brought a few more checks our way and arranged a few more miracles to provide what we needed. But that day I finally felt like there was some light at the end of the tunnel.

I share that story because I can't think of a period in my life when I had to make more decisions than during those two years. Not just regular decisions either—big decisions. Weighty decisions. The kind of decisions that felt like they had everything riding on them, with each one coming down heavier than the last.

The bottom line is that decisions can be stressful. Any decision. Yes, it's true that bigger decisions can lead to more stress, but, really, every decision we have to make is a stressor that lands squarely on our shoulders.

The question is whether we allow those stressors to develop into stress or we turn to God and seek His peace.

Wise and Unwise

It's hard to think of a worse decision than what happened on January 13, 2018. At 8:06 in the morning, every resident of Hawaii received the following emergency text on their phones: "BALLISTIC MISSILE THREAT INBOUND TO HAWAII. SEEK IMMEDIATE SHELTER. THIS IS NOT A DRILL." This was during a season of strong tension between the United States and North Korea.

Of course, the people of Hawaii panicked. Many rushed to find some kind of shelter, even climbing down manholes into sewer systems. Others tried desperately to find relatives or make phone calls during what they believed to be their final minutes on earth.

It wasn't until thirty-eight minutes later, at 8:44, that a second message alerted the public it was all a mistake. There was no threat. The emergency message was supposed to be an exercise—a fire drill of sorts—sent only to employees at the Hawaii Emergency Management Agency. The person who sent out the original message either believed the threat was real or made a mistake in which button they pushed. Either way, it was a terrible decision.[1]

Really, that's what our stress about decision-making boils down to: fear of making the wrong decision. Most of us don't mind decisions in general, and all of us are thrilled when we make a good decision—one that pays off. But when we're confronted with that opportunity to choose, it's easy to become worried about making a bad decision. A decision that will have consequences for not only us but others as well. An unwise decision.

Those fears are justified. The book of Proverbs offers several negative impacts that can come our way when we make bad decisions. Here are some examples:

- *People get hurt.* "Where there is no guidance the people fall" (11:14).
- *Relationships are broken.* "Through overconfidence comes nothing but strife" (13:10).
- *We experience unintended consequence.* "A companion of fools will suffer harm" (13:20).
- *We lose sight of proper boundaries.* "Where there is no vision, the people are unrestrained" (29:18).
- *We damage our character.* "A fool is arrogant and careless" (14:16).

The simple truth is that all decisions have consequences, and unwise decisions have negative consequences.

Does that mean we need to resign ourselves to becoming stressed out whenever we make big decisions? No! There is a solution. To find it, let's look again at those four proverbs, except this time I'll include the whole verse:

- "Where there is no guidance the people fall,
    But in an abundance of counselors there is victory" (11:14).
- "Through overconfidence comes nothing but strife,
    But wisdom is with those who receive counsel" (13:10).
- "One who walks with wise men will be wise,
    But a companion of fools will suffer harm" (13:20).
- "Where there is no vision, the people are unrestrained,
    But happy is one who keeps the Law" (29:18).
- "A wise person is cautious and turns away from evil,
    But a fool is arrogant and careless" (14:16).

Do you see the solution? It's wisdom. When we have wisdom, we're able to discern between good decisions and bad decisions. When we have wisdom, we make wise decisions—which is a great way to eliminate stressors and experience God's peace.

So how do we get wisdom, and how do we make wise decisions? I'll spend the rest of this chapter focusing on two answers to those questions. First, we make wise decisions by saturating ourselves in God's Word. Second, we make wise decisions by seeking wise counsel in our lives.

Saturating Ourselves in God's Word

Way back when I was in middle school, I had a youth pastor who sat me down one day and said, "Vance, did you know there are thirty-one chapters in the book of Proverbs?"

I didn't know that at that point in my life. I didn't even know where to find Proverbs in the Bible. But I said, "Uh-huh."

Then this youth pastor said, "Vance, most months have either thirty or thirty-one days. So I challenge you to read a chapter from Proverbs every day that corresponds with the day of the month. And I challenge you to do that for the rest of your life."

I'm not sure why I accepted that challenge, but I did. I went a whole month reading a chapter a day. Then two months. Then a year. And even now, more than thirty years after I accepted that challenge, I still haven't stopped. If it's the twelfth day of the month, I read Proverbs 12 as part of my quiet time with God. If it's the twenty-seventh, I read Proverbs 27. In fact, if you were to look at any of the Bibles I have used over the years, I guarantee you'll find notes and underlining and messages and wrinkled pages all through the book of Proverbs.

Why have I kept up that habit for all these years? Because of how much it has benefited my life. In fact, I'd say there's no book or passage in the Bible that's changed or spoken into my life more than the book of Proverbs. Saturating myself in God's wisdom has given me a confidence that goes way beyond my own abilities, and it has played a huge part in my experiencing God's peace in a way that is far beyond my ability to comprehend.

Warren Wiersbe writes, "In Proverbs, the words *wise* and *wisdom* are used at least 125 times, because the aim of the book is to help us acquire and apply God's wisdom to the decisions and activities of daily life."[2] So, if you want to eliminate some stress from your life by making wise decisions, I recommend you start exactly where I started: read a chapter from Proverbs every day. Make that a foundational part of your fellowship with Christ as He lives in you and through you.

Of course, I don't recommend you stop at Proverbs. The entire Bible is God's revelation of Himself to humanity, which means the entire Bible is a source of wisdom. As many people have noted over the years, "Nothing less than a whole Bible can make a whole Christian."

Our Attitude toward Scripture

The first step toward gaining wisdom and making wise decisions is saturating ourselves in God's Word. This is a truth that most Christians know. We're aware that we're supposed to read the Bible every day. Sadly, this is also a truth most Christians ignore.

Why is that? One answer is that we have the wrong attitude toward God's Word. Many of us look at Scripture the same way we look at the vitamins in our kitchen cabinets. We see the Bible as a helpful supplement for a happy life.

> The first step toward gaining wisdom and making wise decisions is saturating ourselves in God's Word.

That attitude needs to change, because in reality the Bible is the foundation for the life of a Jesus follower. Through His Word, God invites us daily to sit at His feet and discover the riches of His wisdom. The Bible must be our foundation if we want Christ to live through us in a way that produces fruit for His kingdom—and in a way that allows us to be filled with God's peace.

Here's what Proverbs has to say about this subject:

> My son, comply with the commandment of your
> father,
> And do not ignore the teaching of your mother;
> Bind them continually on your heart;
> Tie them around your neck.
> When you walk, they will guide you;
> When you sleep, they will watch over you;
> And when you awake, they will talk to you.
> For the commandment is a lamp and the teaching is
> light;
> And rebukes for discipline are the way of life.
> (6:20–23)

It's important to remember that Proverbs was often written from the perspective of a father passing wisdom and instruction to his son. And because the ancient world was an oral culture, the idea presented in verse 20 is that of parents passing down the priceless truths of God's Word from one generation to the next.

Two phrases in this passage really summarize what our attitude should be as we approach the Bible. The first phrase is, "Bind them continually on your heart" (v. 21). The word *bind* in the original language meant to tie something together. The idea is attaching something strongly or permanently.

If you know someone who has a pacemaker, that's a great example of something being "bound" to their heart. In that case, a medical device is attached to the heart to keep it functioning well and to bless the person with life. In the same way, we, as Jesus followers, must bind God's Word to our hearts so we can receive life and wisdom from God.

Notice also that this isn't a onetime event. Instead, the verse says, "Bind them continually." The word translated "continually" means ongoing. Never stopping. Our attitude toward God's Word should be to continually treasure the wisdom we find in Scripture. We should continually seek out that wisdom and connect it to ourselves so that it becomes a part of who we are.

I want to rephrase what I just said because it's important: you can't microwave this process of saturating yourself in God's Word. Too many Jesus followers will ignore Scripture for weeks and months, then jump into the Bible with both feet when a problem rears its head—meaning when they feel stressed. That just doesn't work. You can't blindly flip open your Bible, point to a specific verse, and hope that word from God will solve your problem. It won't. Instead, you need to live with God's Word consistently. You need to make it part of you. Saturate yourself with it.

There's a passage from the book of Isaiah that illustrates this principle in a powerful way:

> For as the rain and the snow come down from heaven,
> And do not return there without watering the earth
> And making it produce and sprout,

And providing seed to the sower and bread to the
eater;
So will My word be which goes out of My mouth;
It will not return to Me empty,
Without accomplishing what I desire,
And without succeeding in the purpose for which I
sent it. (55:10–11)

Notice that God's Word sometimes works like rain, and
sometimes it works like snow. That's interesting because
rain and snow ultimately accomplish the same thing—they
water the earth—but they do it in different ways. When it
rains, everything gets wet right away. Immediately. But snow
can sit for weeks or even months before it finally melts and
saturates the soil.

Sometimes, God wants to build a snowbank in our lives.
He wants to pile up His Word and His wisdom so that,
at just the right moment—just when we need it—the Holy
Spirit melts God's truth into our hearts and helps us find His
indescribable peace. For that to happen, though, we need to
consistently expose ourselves to the truth of Scripture.

What does that look like practically? First, it means spending daily time in God's Word as part of our fellowship with
Jesus. Remember all the way back to chapter 1: if we want to
experience God's peace, we need to live each day in constant
fellowship with Christ. A big part of that means saturating ourselves daily in His Word. Second, it means spending
time weekly in God's Word through preaching and teaching.
It means submitting ourselves to the instruction of God's
Word. And third, it means seeking consistent fellowship
with others, centered on God's Word. That means allowing

Scripture to be a regular part of our conversations as we do life with others, both with our friends and family members and as part of a small group from church. All three of these elements are how you can continually bind God's Word to your heart, and that's what it takes if you want to make wise decisions.

The second phrase that stands out is, "And do not ignore the teaching" (Prov. 6:20). The idea is pretty simple: it's one thing to be in the Word, under the Word, and around the Word of God—but it's something else to actively and obediently apply God's Word to your life.

In other words, it's not enough to simply know what the Bible says. You won't receive all the benefits you could receive from Scripture if you simply read it or hear it without also choosing to apply it.

The apostle James, who was Jesus's brother, states this principle as well as anyone ever has:

> But prove yourselves doers of the word, and not just hearers who deceive themselves. For if anyone is a hearer of the word and not a doer, he is like a man who looks at his natural face in a mirror; for once he has looked at himself and gone away, he has immediately forgotten what kind of person he was. But one who has looked intently at the perfect law, the law of freedom, and has continued in it, not having become a forgetful hearer but an active doer, this person will be blessed in what he does. (James 1:22–25)

Don't just listen to God's Word—don't "ignore" its teachings. Instead, in genuine submission to God, follow what His Word says.

Our Reward from Scripture

Right now, you might be wondering, *What's in it for me? If I adjust my attitude toward God's Word, what can I hope to receive?* That's a natural question, and we can look right back to Proverbs 6 to find the answer:

> When you walk, they will guide you;
> When you sleep, they will watch over you;
> And when you awake, they will talk to you.
> For the commandment is a lamp and the teaching is
> light;
> And rebukes for discipline are the way of life. (vv.
> 22–23)

The first thing to see here is that, when we saturate ourselves in God's Word, He will show us the right way to go in life. The more we engage and apply the Scriptures, the better we'll understand which is the right way to go.

Notice how comprehensive those first three lines are. Whenever we walk, the truths of Scripture will "guide" us. Whenever we sleep, "they will watch over" us. Meaning there's an element of protection when we saturate ourselves in God's Word. And when we wake up, those commandments from God's Word "will talk to" us. Meaning there's a relational aspect as well. The better we know and understand God's Word, the better we'll know and understand Jesus and the deeper we'll grow our relationship with Him.

But what especially catches my attention from this passage is the allusion to light: "For the commandment is a lamp and the teaching is light." That may sound similar to another, more famous passage of Scripture from Psalm 119, which says,

> Your word is a lamp to my feet
> And a light to my path. (v. 105)

In other words, one of the main rewards we receive when we saturate ourselves in God's Word is that it helps us see the right path forward. Through His Word, God shows us the way.

One thing you have to deal with when you grow up in Alabama is tornadoes. They are very common. In fact, Alabama and Kansas together have more F5 tornadoes than any other place in the world. And Alabama alone is one of the few places in the world that has multiple tornado seasons. So you just learn to live with that threat constantly out there on the horizon.

If you don't have a lot of experience with tornadoes, another thing that typically accompanies them and the storms that produce them is power outages. During my time in Alabama, it was very common for a big storm to come through, the tornado warning sirens to start blaring—and then for the power to be gone. Just cut off in an instant.

Now, when the power goes out in Las Vegas, where I live now, it gets dark. But there's a big difference between city dark and country dark. Because when the power went out in Alabama as a kid, I remember it being Dark with a capital *D*. Thick, black storm clouds. Trees overhanging everything. There was no moon visible, no stars, and everything was just opaque, both outside and inside. Fortunately, most people in Alabama prepare for this by having three or four places in their homes where they store flashlights and candles.

Here's something I learned from a young age: when it gets dark, if you can't access a light, you're in big trouble.

The same is true when it comes to making decisions. If you're trying to make decisions in the dark, you're in trouble. If you're trying to make decisions using your own resources, your own intelligence, and your own approximation of wisdom, you're in trouble. You won't know the right way to go, which means you'll feel a lot of stress, both before and after the decision gets made.

The solution, then, is to turn on the light. Many people, even many Jesus followers, are mired in fear, anxiety, confusion, and stress because they don't seek God daily through His Word. They don't take advantage of their access to His light, then they wonder why they don't know what to do or where to go.

If you want to make wise decisions, saturate yourself in God's Word. Because that Word will be a light to show you the way.

Proverbs 6:23 shows a second reward we receive when we focus on the Bible: "And rebukes for discipline are the way of life." This verse has two key words. First, *rebukes* in the original language meant to correct something that was wrong. It's a similar idea to that of a parent reproving a child who has misbehaved. The other term is *discipline*, which had a different meaning in the original language than the one we typically use today. We think of discipline as punishment. In the world of the Old Testament, however, discipline was more accurately a form of instruction. Think of a coach correcting an athlete's poor technique.

So, the first reward we receive from saturating ourselves in God's Word is that His light will show us the right way to go. The second is that Scripture will correct us whenever we start going the wrong way.

Both those blessings will help us make wise decisions and minimize the number of stressors that pile on our shoulders from the fear of making unwise decisions.

Seeking Wise Counsel

So far in this chapter, I've made a big deal about Proverbs being a fount of wisdom within God's Word. It's worth asking the question, then, What does Proverbs say about finding wisdom and making wise decisions?

Well, Proverbs says quite a bit. In fact, there's a dominant theme that runs through almost every chapter when it comes to how people can be wise and make good decisions. Let me give you a few examples of what I mean, and let's see if you can catch the theme. Here they are:

> Where there is no guidance the people fall,
> But in an abundance of counselors there is victory.
> (11:14)

> The way of a fool is right in his own eyes,
> But a person who listens to advice is wise. (12:15)

> One who walks with wise people will be wise,
> But a companion of fools will suffer harm. (13:20)

> Listen to advice and accept discipline,
> So that you may be wise the rest of your days. (19:20)

> For by wise guidance you will wage war,
> And in an abundance of counselors there is victory.
> (24:6)

Do you see the dominant theme? Here it is in a nutshell: if we want to make wise decisions, we need to seek godly counsel. And I'm not talking about professional counselors here—pastors included. I'm talking about our personal relationships. If we want to make wise decisions, we need to invite godly people who know us well and are allowed to tell us the truth into our decision-making.

Look back at Proverbs 12:15:

> The way of a fool is right in his own eyes,
> But a person who listens to advice is wise.

I was praying about that verse years ago when I wrote three statements in my Bible that have stayed with me ever since:

1. My input is never enough because I don't know everything.
2. My perspective is always limited because I can't see everything.
3. My flesh is always deceitful because my own heart will lie to me about anything.

The bottom line is that, left to myself, I am more than capable of making wrong decisions. Bad decisions. Even horrible decisions. The same is true for you. Therefore, the wise thing for each of us to do is to be honest and humble about our own limitations.

We need God's guidance in our lives if we want to make wise decisions. And as we've already seen, one way we can receive that guidance is by saturating ourselves in His Word. But it's also true that God often speaks to us and guides us through the counsel we receive from godly women and men who allow Christ to live and speak through them.

So let's conclude this chapter by looking at three ways we can seek godly counsel from others as a key ingredient in making wise decisions that will eliminate stress from our lives and allow us to experience God's indescribable peace.

Establish Relationships with Godly People

Here's a question worth considering: Who influences your life the most? Is it your spouse? A parent? Your best friend or a group of friends? Or a better way to ask that question might be this: Who are you choosing to give the most influence in your life? Because sometimes you don't have a choice. You don't always get to choose your boss, for example, but they may gain a lot of influence in your life. The same can be true of coworkers, neighbors, teachers, and so on.

Bottom line, who are you allowing to have the most influence in your life? And is their influence leading you toward godliness and wise decisions—or something else?

I ask these questions because Proverbs 13:20 is true:

> One who walks with wise people will be wise,
> But a companion of fools will suffer harm.

Meaning the people you invite into your life will either lead you toward wisdom or lead you toward foolishness. There isn't a third direction.

I had an aha moment as I was studying this verse because I realized that wise decision-making begins long before a decision actually falls into my lap. The circumstances of my life are constantly creating the environment out of which

I make decisions—and that includes the people I allow to influence my life and speak into my decisions. Therefore, my relational choices establish the environment from which my decisions are made.

Anyone who has been a parent of a teenager understands this principle. When our kids are around other kids who make bad decisions, our kids start making bad decisions. But we don't always understand that the same is true of us.

Charles Stanley says it this way: "You will become wise by associating with people who are wise, or you will suffer the painful consequences of imprudent relationships."[3]

Now, you might be wondering, *Does that mean I shouldn't develop any friendships with people who are unbelievers or people who are not godly?* No, that's not what I'm saying. We have been commanded by Christ to "go, therefore, and make disciples" (Matt. 28:19), which means we have a responsibility to connect relationally with those who are unsaved or even immature in their faith.

But that does not mean we should give those people permission to speak into our own lives in a major way. That level of influence should be extended only to those we know are godly and will lead us toward wisdom.

So the first step in looking for wise counsel is to actively and intentionally seek godly people who have wisdom, then invite those people into our lives through relationships.

Lean on Those Relationships for Input

Our second step is to actively and intentionally seek input from those relationships when we need to make a decision—and to actually listen to what those godly people have to say. Because it's one thing to simply have healthy relationships in place. It's another thing to be intentional about maximizing those relationships and seeking counsel when it's time to make a decision.

There's something I say all the time to our staff at Hope Church. In fact, the people who work with me are probably sick and tired of hearing the same phrase, but I plan to keep on saying it anyway. Here it is: *Don't make decisions on an island.* Why? Because we always make better decisions together.

What we sometimes don't understand is that it takes discipline to seek input from others. When it comes time to make a decision, there are often many reasons to not get others involved. Maybe we think we already know what they'll say. Maybe we don't want to bother people. Maybe we feel like there isn't time to get input—we just need to make the decision and move on.

Those are all bad reasons for making bad decisions. What we need to do is build into our lives the discipline of seeking input before we make decisions. And not just seeking input but actually listening to it.

Think about that point for a moment. When people take the time to speak into your life and offer counsel, do you listen? Of course, it's easy to listen when people agree with us. But when others try pointing us in a different direction, we often immediately default to justifying ourselves and thinking about all the reasons we're right and they don't really understand. Such justifications don't lead to wise decisions, however; they lead to stress. Therefore, we need to genuinely consider the counsel we receive from others.

Warren Wiersbe puts it this way: "In seeking counsel, we must be sincere, because a loving and wise friend can often see dangers and detours that are hidden from us."[4]

Choose to Be Teachable

Seeking wise counsel involves establishing relationships with godly people and choosing to receive input from those people. And finally, it requires us to be teachable. Meaning we need to be open to the idea that we might be wrong, and we need to accept ideas, plans, or decisions that didn't come from our own minds.

Do you know what I've learned after decades of studying the Bible? I've learned the Bible is in-your-face true. I always knew the Bible was true; I grew up in church, after all. But the more I have dug in and saturated myself in the truth of God's Word, the more I realize the Word pulls no punches. Scripture is unafraid to hit me in the mouth because God knows I need it. With that in mind, let me finish this chapter by guiding you through two in-your-face verses from the book of Proverbs.

Here's the first one:

> The way of a fool is right in his own eyes,
> But a wise man is he who listens to counsel. (12:15
> NASB1995)

If you think the Bible just called you a fool, you're probably right. It also called me a fool, because I am certainly vulnerable to believing myself to be right most of the time. That's natural, given our human nature, but it's not helpful for making wise decisions and removing stress from our lives. If you pretty much always think you're correct, you're acting foolishly. That's an in-your-face truth, but it's true.

And look at the next part of the verse. It doesn't say people are wise who *seek* counsel; it says the wise person "listens to counsel." The word *listens* means to place yourself under the counsel of another. To give real attention to the instruction of others, and even to the correction of others. To make wise decisions, we need to be teachable.

Here's the second in-your-face verse about listening to correction:

> Whoever loves discipline loves knowledge,
> But he who hates reproof is stupid. (12:1 NASB1995)

Did you ever think the Bible would call someone stupid? There it is.

In the seventeenth century, a Bible scholar named Albert Barnes wrote a commentary on Scripture. When he got to Proverbs 12, he paid some special attention to this verse. Specifically, the word translated as "stupid" above he translated as "dumb as an ox." That's what that Hebrew term meant in the original language.

What does it mean to hate reproof? It means doing everything we can to avoid correction. It means ignoring wise and godly people around you, and it means rejecting what those people say. As we mentioned earlier, the word translated "discipline" in that verse does not mean punishment; rather, it means instruction. So, according to the Bible, people who refuse to listen to instruction or correction are dumb as an ox.

The outcome of everything I'm saying here is that failing to seek and heed godly counsel will result in unwise decisions—which, in turn, will result in stress.

Thankfully, you don't have to go that way. You can grow in wisdom by saturating yourself in God's Word, which is filled with His wisdom. And you can set up helpful guardrails around your decision-making by not only seeking out wise and godly people to offer you instruction and advice but also listening to what they have to say—and even accepting correction and reproof when you're pushing yourself in the wrong direction.

You're always going to have decisions that you have to make. That's inevitable. But those decisions don't need to lead to stress. Instead, you can operate with the confidence of God's wisdom, which in turn will help you live a stressless life by filling you with God's peace.

7

Guard Your Heart

How Do I Cling to God's Peace in the Face of Spiritual Attack?

If you had to identify the most influential people in human history, what names would be on your list? Yes, I think you and I would both start with Jesus at number one, but who then? That's a question people could spend a lot of time arguing about.

Back in the early 2000s, a Pulitzer Prize–winning historian named Arthur Schlesinger Jr. decided to put together his own list, although the time line was a little narrower. Writing for the *World Almanac*, Schlesinger identified the most influential people of the second millennium—the years between 1000 and 1999.

Here is his list:

1. William Shakespeare
2. Isaac Newton

3. Charles Darwin
4. Nicolaus Copernicus
5. Galileo Galilei
6. Albert Einstein
7. Christopher Columbus
8. Abraham Lincoln
9. Johannes Gutenberg
10. William Harvey[1]

As I was reading through that list the first time, I patted myself on the back for knowing each name as it came up. I consider myself a student of history, so I was nodding along with the article. *Shakespeare, yep. "To be or not to be." Copernicus changed our understanding of the universe. Einstein had the theory of general relativity, sure. Gutenberg built the first printing press, okay.*

Then I came to number ten on the list. *William Harvey? Who in the world is that?* I'll admit, I was a little affronted that someone could be one of the ten most influential people of the past thousand years without me ever hearing about him. So I did some research, and it turns out Arthur Schlesinger Jr. might know a little bit more about history than I do.

William Harvey was a medical doctor who practiced in the early 1600s. Before his time, the medical establishment believed that human bodies converted food into blood within the liver. Then that blood was sent to the heart, where it was heated and pumped to other sections of the body through the veins (rather than the arteries).

Obviously, the medical consensus was wrong. Big time. Thankfully, that consensus changed because of the work of

William Harvey. Specifically, Harvey was the first person to show in detail that the human circulatory system begins and ends with the heart. In fact, everything we know today about cardiovascular health and fighting heart disease can be traced back to William Harvey's discoveries. So, yes, William Harvey was an incredibly influential person. Because when it comes to our everyday lives, what's more important than the heart?

Thankfully, we can do many things to protect our hearts in a physical sense. We can eat right, even if that means cutting back on salt and steak and other delicious foods. (My wife keeps telling me it does.) We can exercise. We can find a doctor we trust and submit to regular exams. In short, we can be intentional about removing factors that will harm us so we can live stressless lives through God's peace.

That's similar to the theme we've been exploring for several chapters now. We've seen there are many areas of life that are especially prone to throwing stressors on our shoulders—our schedules, finances, relationships, decisions, and so on. We've identified ways to remove these stressors so they don't produce stress and we can instead be filled with God's peace.

In this chapter, we're going to look at the stressors that are more targeted at our inner lives—the core of who we are and our relationship with Jesus—and are therefore all the more dangerous.

After all, as William Harvey showed us centuries ago, what's more important than the heart?

Keep Watch

Dr. Harvey was one of the first to realize the importance of the heart in our physical lives, but Scripture had him beat by a couple thousand years. Several passages address the critical nature of our hearts, but one of my favorites comes from the book of Proverbs.

> Watch over your heart with all diligence,
> For from it flow the springs of life.
> Rid yourself of a deceitful mouth
> And keep devious speech far from you.
> Let your eyes look directly ahead
> And let your gaze be fixed straight in front of you.
> Watch the path of your feet,
> And all your ways will be established.
> Do not turn to the right or to the left;
> Turn your foot from evil. (4:23–27)

We're going to dig into that entire passage before we finish this chapter, but for right now I want to focus on those first two lines. The New Living Translation phrases them this way:

> Guard your heart above all else,
> for it determines the course of your life. (v. 23)

If we want to eliminate stress from our lives, and if we want to experience the full measure of God's peace, then we'll need to guard or keep watch over our hearts.

Now, the Hebrew word translated as "heart" in verse 23 is obviously not the blood-pumping organ found in your chest. Instead, whenever the Bible talks about your heart, it's pointing to the real you. It's pointing to who you are on the inside. From a biblical perspective, your heart is the seat of your mind, your will, and your emotions. It's the sum total of your moral and spiritual life, especially in the context of your relationship with God.

It goes without saying, then, that our hearts are important! Our hearts are incredibly valuable. That's why Scripture says we must "guard" or "watch over" them.

Just outside of Colorado Springs, Colorado, lies the Cheyenne Mountain Air Force Station, which many people believe to be the most secure military facility in the entire world. The station was originally designed as the primary base of operations for North American Aerospace Defense Command, or NORAD, and the bunker was carved out under two thousand feet of granite with the express intention of surviving a nuclear attack. The entire facility can be sealed off by two concrete and steel blast doors, both of which are three and a half feet thick and weigh twenty-three tons.[2]

Why is the Cheyenne Mountain Air Force Station so heavily reinforced and carefully protected? Because it houses both people and technology that are critical for the proper functioning of our nation.

That's the same idea communicated by the author of Proverbs. He said to "watch over your heart with all diligence." In other words, guard your heart above all else! Why? Because "from it flow the springs of life." Or back to the NLT, because your heart "determines the course of your life."

The overall idea is that we have been given something precious: the gift of life. We've been given the opportunity to not just exist—to not just punch a time card, watch some TV, and maybe do something nice for others every now and again—but to participate in God's eternal plans and purposes for the universe. We've been given the opportunity to live and find joy and purpose as members of God's kingdom. And this opportunity starts and flows out of our hearts. Therefore, we're commanded to guard our hearts. To treasure and value that opportunity. To protect it.

Now, remember that every time God commands us to do something in Scripture, it's for our good. He created us, He loves us, and He knows what's best for us. So when He says to us, "Do this," what He's really saying is, "Help yourself by doing this." When He says to us, "Don't do that," what He's really saying is, "Don't hurt yourself by doing that."

The same thing is true here. The essence of who we are and the direction of our lives flow out of our hearts, which means everything about us can be affected by what we allow to touch our hearts. Whatever influences us internally will impact the core of who we are, and the direction of our lives—whether that impact is good or bad.

For example, think of a computer. There's no shortage of harmful people who want to send harmful things to your computer—viruses, malware, spam, tracking programs, and more. If you allow those destructive programs to come in, they will quickly affect how your computer operates on the inside, which will quickly produce negative consequences in your life. If you're lucky, you'll just get a bunch of spam emails. If you're unlucky, you may end up having your most personal data sold to the worst kind of people and credit cards opened up in your name without your knowledge. The old-school way of describing this idea is "garbage in, garbage out." When we allow harmful things to influence our hearts, we will be harmed.

However, if you protect your computer—if you install the right antivirus software and make sure everything is updated on a regular basis—your computer will do all the things it's supposed to do and be a productive tool for your life.

So here's the principle that will serve as the foundation for the rest of this chapter: *you can prevent or reduce stress in your life by carefully guarding what you allow to influence your heart.* This principle works on the flip side as well: *when you aren't careful about guarding what you allow to influence your heart, you will increase the amount of stress in your life.*

> You can prevent or reduce stress in your life by carefully guarding what you allow to influence your heart.

We will go in either one of those directions. Thankfully, we have a choice. And I want to show you in the following pages how to remove stressors that may have piled up on your shoulders because you haven't been guarding your heart.

See the Enemy

Right about now you might be asking, *Guard my heart from what, exactly? What's the big threat that I need to keep watch against to protect myself?*

Those are great questions, and the answers are both simple and complex. I say the answers are simple because they can be boiled down to one word: *Satan.* The reason you need to guard your heart is because you have an enemy; you're under attack. I say the answers are complex because there's a lot of confusion and wishful thinking in the world today—and even in the church—when it comes to the nature and methods of this enemy. A lot needs to be cleared up.

Let's take a moment to focus on our enemy, the devil. You could fill entire libraries with all the books that have been written about Satan and spiritual warfare, so we don't have time to be exhaustive in our focus. Instead, I want to highlight three truths about Satan that have a direct application to living a stressless life and choosing to be filled with God's peace.

Satan Is Real

Our family used to play a lot of board games when our children were growing up, and one of my favorites was Risk. If you're not familiar with that game, the premise is simple: conquer the world. Each player occupies different nations across the world map, and each player starts with an army spread across those nations. Once the game starts, it's all-out war. Conquer or be conquered.

Sometimes we'd have a game during which one of the kids (or maybe one of their friends) was a little too young to really understand what was going on. They'd have fun playing with their little army pieces or rolling the dice, but they had no real concept of being in a fight and no real ability to set up a military strategy. I'd try to have mercy in such situations—but my older kids never did. Without fail, the unfortunate combatant would be wiped out and sent packing in just a few turns.

Tragically, a similar dynamic is at play in the world today when people, especially Jesus followers, don't realize they're in a battle—when they don't realize they're living in the middle of a war. Why don't they realize it? Because they don't think Satan or his forces are real.

In a recent survey conducted by the Barna Group, 56 percent of Americans agreed with the statement that "Satan is not merely a symbol of evil but is a real spiritual being and influences human lives."[3] That number was actually up from a similar survey conducted ten years before, which is good news. Still, 44 percent of Americans disagreed with that statement. Almost half the country. Those people don't understand they're under attack and in danger of being wiped out.

Let me set the record straight: you cannot believe the Bible is true and not believe Satan is real and out to destroy you. In the New Testament alone, the word *Satan* is mentioned thirty-six times and *devil* is mentioned thirty-four times. (To give some context, Mary, Jesus's mother, is mentioned only twenty times.) Every New Testament author talks about Satan as a real being and our enemy. Jesus talked about the devil too—a lot.

The devil is real. But who is he? What is he? And what does he want? Scripture gives us insight into those questions as well.

First, we need to understand that Satan is a fallen angel. The prophet Ezekiel is referring to Satan when he writes, "You were blameless in your ways from the day you were created until unrighteousness was found in you. By the abundance of your trade you were internally filled with violence, and you sinned; therefore I have cast you as profane from the mountain of God. And I have destroyed you, you covering cherub, from the midst of the stones of fire" (Ezek. 28:15–16).

This is important because many people view Satan as the opposite of God. They see God and Satan as a kind of yin and yang—equal powers locked in eternal combat. That's not the case. God is the Creator; Satan was created. God is all-powerful; Satan is powerful, yes, but limited. God is present everywhere and knows everything; Satan is a spiritual being, which means he's different from human beings, but he's still limited in what he knows and where he can be.

We also need to understand that Satan has real power within our world. Jesus called him "the ruler of this world" (John 12:31). Paul referred to Satan as "the god of this world" (2 Cor. 4:4). Notice the small g, of course. Why does Satan have so much power over our world? Because of sin. When God created Adam and Eve, He gave humanity dominion over creation. God put us in charge. But when Adam and Eve rebelled against God through their sin, the world itself became corrupted by sin, which means the world is temporarily under the control of Satan.

And it's not only Satan but also other spiritual beings under his command who exert power in our world. Paul writes, "For our struggle is not against flesh and blood, but against the rulers, against the powers, against the world forces of this darkness, against the spiritual forces of wickedness in the heavenly places" (Eph. 6:12). These forces are spiritual beings (former angels) who joined Satan in his rebellion against God and were cast out of heaven along with him. We typically refer to them as demons or evil spirits.

John MacArthur offers some explanation for these beings: "Satan's forces of darkness are highly organized and structured for the most destructive warfare possible. . . . They are a great and ancient multitude and constitute a formidable and highly experienced supernatural enemy."[4] In other words, Satan has an army. And he uses that army to fight against God's plans and purposes for the world by directly attacking those of us who have surrendered our lives to Christ.

Make no mistake: if we're seeking to live the life of a Jesus follower—and especially if we want to experience God's peace—Satan has us in his sights. He'll attack us, and his goal isn't merely to make us feel stressed out. His goal is total domination. Total destruction. Peter writes, "Be of sober spirit, be on the alert. Your adversary, the devil, prowls around like a roaring lion, seeking someone to devour" (1 Pet. 5:8).

Have you ever been flipping through the channels on TV and stumbled onto one of those Discovery Channel shows where a lion or some other big predator is stalking its prey? You never want to be the gazelle in that scenario, right? When you see the camera pan to the herd, you already know it's not going to end well for one lonely gazelle. And when the lion catches its prey? Well, that's what Peter meant when he used the word in Scripture translated "devour." It's violent. It's vicious. And it ends in total devastation. You see, Satan is playing a game of Risk for the world, and he wants to utterly and completely destroy us.

> Make no mistake: if we're seeking to live the life of a Jesus follower—and especially if we want to experience God's peace—Satan has us in his sights.

In short, one of the very real causes of stressors and stress is the reality that we're in the middle of a war. We're under attack every single day of our lives. Because Satan and his forces are as real as a lion prowling the plain on a sunny day.

Satan Is a Liar

The second truth about Satan that I want to highlight is that he's a liar to the core. Deception is his default operating system. In the words of Jesus, "[Satan] was a murderer from the beginning, and does not stand in the truth because there is no truth in him. Whenever he tells a lie, he speaks from his own nature, because he is a liar and the father of lies" (John 8:44).

In other words, as we engage in spiritual battle against Satan and his forces, we should never expect a fair fight. Our adversary will always fight dirty.

Specifically, our adversary will seek out our weaknesses through observation. Back to Ephesians 6, Paul warned Christians to "put on the full armor of God, so that you will be able to stand firm against the schemes of the devil" (v. 11). That word translated "schemes" means methods or plans that are premeditated. The picture is of an intentional strategy based on observation.

Have you noticed how some of the strongest temptations hit you right at your weakest moments? Wouldn't you say you've made some of your worst decisions when you were compromised in some way—when you were tired, lonely, angry, or even just hungry? Those things didn't happen by accident. Your spiritual enemies have observed you for a long time, and they know when you're most vulnerable to attack.

Once Satan and his forces gain a good understanding of us by observing our weaknesses, they attack by exploiting those weaknesses through deception. That deception usually comes in one of three forms.

First, our adversaries attack through distortion by twisting the truth in an attempt to use it against us. *Why would God try to stop me from doing something that feels good? Didn't my pastor say just last week that God wants me to be happy?*

Second, our enemies attack us through doubt by working to make us question the truth. This usually happens when we're hit by suffering or negative circumstances. *Would a good God really allow something like this to happen? What makes me think I can really trust God to watch out for me?* Or the attack may come internally and be connected to our failures. *How could God love me when I fail Him so often?*

Third, our spiritual enemies attack us with distraction by trying to lead us away from the truth. A practical example from my life is that I've noticed distractions often arise right when I'm preparing to spend time in fellowship with Jesus. The phone rings. There's a knock on my office door. Internally, I'm distracted by a problem I need to solve or a point I'm trying to get right in an upcoming sermon. I've noticed in my conversations with many Christians today that smartphones are especially dangerous sources of distraction—they beep or buzz or bing at just the wrong moment. None of these distractions are coincidences; they are attacks.

Looking at Scripture, the temptation of Eve in the garden of Eden is a textbook example of our adversaries' methods when it comes to spiritual attack. Here's the passage:

> Now the serpent was more cunning than any animal of the field which the LORD God had made. And he said to the

woman, "Has God really said, 'You shall not eat from any tree of the garden'?" The woman said to the serpent, "From the fruit of the trees of the garden we may eat; but from the fruit of the tree which is in the middle of the garden, God has said, 'You shall not eat from it or touch it, or you will die.'" The serpent said to the woman, "You certainly will not die! For God knows that on the day you eat from it your eyes will be opened, and you will become like God, knowing good and evil." When the woman saw that the tree was good for food, and that it was a delight to the eyes, and that the tree was desirable to make one wise, she took some of its fruit and ate; and she also gave some to her husband with her, and he ate. (Gen. 3:1–6)

To start, notice that Satan's attack was timed to occur when God wasn't physically present with Adam and Eve in the garden. Satan observed before he attacked, and he exploited a moment of weakness. Also notice that Satan began with distortion: "Has God really said . . . ?" He distorted God's command to avoid one tree as a command to avoid all trees. Then Satan attacked with doubt. When Eve repeated God's warning that eating from the Tree of Knowledge of Good and Evil would result in death, the serpent said, "You certainly will not die!" He even implied God was trying to keep Adam and Eve from experiencing joy.

Let's get back to you. You're in the middle of a war, and your enemy is actively attacking you through all kinds of deception. The goal of those attacks is to harm you—to drive a wedge in your fellowship with God and to destroy you in any and every way possible. That includes increasing the number of stressors you face each day so that you're distracted and crushed down, and that certainly includes doing everything possible to keep you from experiencing God's incomprehensible peace.

That's the bad news.

Satan Is Defeated

The good news in all of this is that Satan has been defeated. The war against evil has been won, and every Jesus follower is already on the winning side.

I've mentioned a few times that I'm a big fan of college football, especially the Alabama Crimson Tide. That's my team. During football season, Saturdays are tense for me when I watch Alabama play live. But all that tension gets ratcheted up 1,000 percent when Alabama plays in the National Championship. Watching those games, the roller coaster is real! I feel joy and elation when the Crimson Tide score a touchdown. I break out in a sweat when the other team does something well or retakes the lead. Everything is intense!

Sometimes, though, I'll watch a recording of an old Alabama victory when I need a little relaxation. That's a totally different experience. If the other team scores a touchdown, I don't blink an eye. Even if Alabama is losing in the fourth quarter, I just laugh because I know what's about to happen.

Do you see the difference? Knowing who wins completely changes the outcome. It lowers my stress and allows me to be at peace no matter what happens.

Well, as Jesus followers, we know who wins this ongoing battle between God and the forces of evil. Jesus does! That's the primary theme of the book of Revelation—not to make us guess who might be the Antichrist but to show us that God wins in the end. The devil may prowl around like a roaring lion, but the Lion of Judah defeated him once and for all when He rose from the grave. Jesus has won!

And if you're wondering how I can be so sure, it's because I've already seen the end of the ball game: "And the devil who deceived them was thrown into the lake of fire and brimstone, where the beast and the false prophet are also; and they will be tormented day and night forever and ever" (Rev. 20:10).

No matter how viciously your enemy attacks you, and no matter how many stressors he tries to pile on top of your life, you don't have to be afraid. You don't have to stress about anything Satan does, nor any of his forces. Instead, you can focus all your efforts on your fellowship with Jesus and embracing His plans for your life—both of which will fill you with peace.

All that's possible because you aren't fighting *for* victory against your enemy. You're fighting *from* victory.

Set the Agenda

When you're faced with a spiritual attack, the first thing you must do is keep watch over your heart to guard the precious gift of life you've been given. The second thing you must do is see your enemy for who he is and understand you're in a war. Finally, because you're fighting that war from the victory Christ has already won, you need to set the agenda when it comes to the day-to-day work of guarding your heart.

What do I mean by "set the agenda"? I mean actively setting a watch over your heart by taking control of your everyday life. Specifically, by preemptively taking control of those areas where temptations and negative influences often arise.

Let's look back at Proverbs 4:23–27:

> Watch over your heart with all diligence,
> For from it flow the springs of life.
> Rid yourself of a deceitful mouth
> And keep devious speech far from you.
> Let your eyes look directly ahead
> And let your gaze be fixed straight in front of you.
> Watch the path of your feet,
> And all your ways will be established.
> Do not turn to the right or to the left;
> Turn your foot from evil.

Remember the context of these verses. The author is very likely Solomon, and he was recording these wisdom sayings as a way of teaching and preparing his own son to enter into adulthood. This entire chapter is a plea from father to son to live wisely and well.

Specifically, Solomon warned his son to guard his heart, and then he explained how to do that in three specific areas of life: our ears, our eyes, and our feet.

Ears

Verse 24 says,

> Rid yourself of a deceitful mouth
> And keep devious speech far from you.

If I could paraphrase that verse in a single phrase, it would be this: be careful what you listen to. And by "listen," I don't necessarily mean words or speech that happen to bounce through your ear canal and end up in your brain. Instead, I mean be careful what you give your attention to. Be careful what you consider. Be careful about the kinds of speech you allow to influence you.

Solomon is reminding us that some things we listen to are dangerous to our hearts and our walk with the Lord. People, words, and ideas can impact us in negative ways if we allow them into our hearts.

Two specific examples are listed in this verse. The first is "a deceitful mouth." This is someone who habitually speaks without integrity. It's the kind of talk that points us toward disobedience or is crooked in some way—it doesn't line up with the truth.

The idea is that we should refuse to listen to people or ideas that don't line up with the truth of God's Word. Solomon says to "rid yourself" of such talk. Obviously, that means we shouldn't speak those kinds of words. But it also means intentionally distancing ourselves from those who do.

The second example is "devious speech." That word translated "devious" means that which is foul, ruined, or unpleasant. Practical examples include obscene language, dirty jokes, racial slurs, gossip, slander, and more.

Have you encountered that kind of speech in the past week? If so, how did you respond? Solomon says you need to keep it "far from you." You need to be careful what you listen to.

Speaking frankly, it's a real challenge to guard our hearts this way in the modern world. When Solomon wrote this advice for his son, everything that could be heard was spoken by another person physically nearby. But in today's world, technology constantly bombards us with all kinds of speech, including that which is deceitful and devious. We're living right now as a generation of people who seem to be walking around with something in our ears just about all the time.

We're hearing more speech today than at any other point in human history, and Solomon is warning us that we need to be careful what we listen to if we want to guard our hearts from harmful influences.

How do we do that? Paul has an answer for us in the book of Philippians: "Finally, brothers and sisters, whatever is true, whatever is honorable, whatever is right, whatever is pure, whatever is lovely, whatever is commendable, if there is any excellence and if anything worthy of praise, think about these things" (4:8).

You need to set the agenda for what you listen to in your life, and you can use this verse as a fantastic filter for what you give attention to each day. Think of everything you listen to on a regular basis—TV shows, podcasts, coworkers, family members, talk radio, music, etc. With each example, ask yourself, "Is this true?" "Is this honorable?" "Is it pure, lovely, commendable, excellent, and worthy of praise?" If so, keep listening. If not, get rid of it.

Because you need to guard your heart if you want a stressless life.

Eyes

Solomon continues with Proverbs 4:25:

> Let your eyes look directly ahead
> And let your gaze be fixed straight in front of you.

What advice was he giving to his son in that verse? To guard his heart from wandering eyes.

There's no doubt that airplanes are a wonderful tool in the modern world. They give us unprecedented access to people and places all over the world. They're critical engines for business. They're also incredibly helpful for sharing the gospel and equipping the global church. However, as we learned through the terrorist attacks of September 11, 2001, a wonderful tool can be turned into a dangerous weapon in the hands of an enemy.

In a similar way, there are many wonderful tools because of technology today that advance what we can see—that give us incredible access to information, education, entertainment, and more. I'm thinking primarily of the internet, of course, but the reality is that there are so many tools today it's hard to keep track: computers, cell phones, cameras, video game systems, virtual reality, and on, and on.

Here's what we need to understand, though: each of those wonderful tools can become a dangerous weapon in the hands of our enemy. This is especially true of the internet and the way it influences our hearts through what we see. In fact, I have a friend who has been a psychologist for over forty years now. He told me the age of the internet has been the greatest onslaught of the enemy against Christian men he has ever witnessed. And it's not hard to understand why. According to the Barna Group, 68 percent of Christian men view pornography regularly. Even among married couples, 55 percent of men say they search for porn once a month. It's not just men either. Among women under the age of twenty-five, 33 percent view porn regularly, and 33 percent of married women search for porn once a month.[5]

This is a huge problem! Why? Because we're allowing the enemy access to our hearts. We're allowing our adversary to gain access through the doorway of our eyes and wreak havoc on the course of our lives.

It's not just pornography, of course. There are many harmful things we can watch and give our attention to. But the internet has put more information and images in front of our eyes in a moment than previous generations could access in a lifetime. Yes, that can be a blessing, but it's more likely to become a curse if we don't actively guard our hearts.

That being said, here are four quick and practical steps you can take to set the agenda for your eyes and the eyes of those in your household.

First, never allow children or teenagers unsupervised access to the internet. For me, this is critical. I still have a teenager in my home, and I don't care what her friends' parents do. I don't care what the culture thinks. It is critical for me that my children do not have unsupervised, unlimited access to the internet.

Sadly, many children and teens do. A recent study showed roughly nine in ten teenagers go online multiple times a day, and 45 percent say they are on the internet "almost constantly." That's according to Pew Research.[6] Worse, 64 percent of young people (ages thirteen to twenty-four) actively seek out pornography weekly or more often.[7]

A huge percentage of young people in today's world, both Christians and non-Christians, have allowed their adversary almost unfettered access to their hearts through the internet.

This is like giving Satan a loaded gun and helping him point it at our children, and we can already see the consequences. Neha Chaudhary, child and adolescent psychiatrist at Massachusetts General Hospital and Harvard Medical School, recently said, "Teen social media use has been thought to be correlated with depression, anxiety, worsening self-esteem, and loneliness."[8]

Now, I'm not recommending you hover over your child's shoulder any time they use the internet. But I am saying they shouldn't have unsupervised access. There need to be checks and balances. The reality is that until children are mature enough to make their own decisions, parents need to set the agenda as the guardians of their hearts.

Second, always filter your content and devices when anyone from your household accesses the internet. And I'm not just talking about kids and teens here. I'm talking about you and me. Plenty of services are available to help you screen out harmful content, so take advantage of those tools to guard your own heart.

Again, this isn't just about pornography. This is about setting the agenda to close off any point of access the enemy may have to your heart.

For example, a little while ago I noticed I was spending too much time on my phone. Sometimes I would just pick it up without even knowing why—I had formed a habit of scrolling through different apps and feeds when I had even a moment of spare time. That wasn't good. That wasn't helpful to me. So I set the agenda. I programmed some limits into the phone with my Screen Time app, then I gave the phone to my wife and asked her to create a passcode. If I use the phone too long, everything shuts down and I can't do a thing for the rest of the day without begging my wife to let me back in.

That points to the third way we can set the agenda for what we see: establish accountability with people we can trust. Solomon said this in the book of Ecclesiastes: "Two are better than one because they have a good return for their labor; for if either of them falls, the one will lift up his companion. But woe to the one who falls when there is not another to lift him up!" (4:9–10). That's accountability, and that's a necessary step if you want to keep watch over your heart.

I have three people in my life who have every password to every device, website, subscription, and app I have access to. They can get into everything I get into. Why? Because I need accountability. And so do you.

> No weapon you and I wield can disrupt the plans of our adversary more than repentance.

Finally, the last step for setting a watch over your heart in terms of what you see is this: if you're already in trouble, seek help. Find someone you can trust, then open up your heart with an honest confession. Don't try to beat this by yourself, because it probably won't work. Instead, there are programs specifically designed to help you find freedom—and they do work. All you have to do is reach out.

Let me say this: no weapon you and I wield can disrupt the plans of our adversary more than repentance. Sin thrives in the shadows—in secret. When we open up the doors and shine the light of God on the darkest corners of our hearts through repentance, we break the enemy's power over us.

The psalmist writes, "I will walk within my house in the integrity of my heart. I will set no worthless thing before my eyes" (Ps. 101:2–3). That's what it means to guard your heart against what you see.

Feet

Solomon pleaded with his son to keep watch over his heart by setting limits on what he listened to, what he saw, and finally, where he went. Where he allowed his feet to take him. Look at Proverbs 4:26–27:

> Watch the path of your feet,
> And all your ways will be established.
> Do not turn to the right or to the left;
> Turn your foot from evil.

There are places a follower of Jesus doesn't belong, and I'm willing to guess you know exactly what those places are in your own life. In my experience, people often put themselves in compromised situations, then try to avoid temptation through willpower. They get close to the edge, *then* try to make a stand.

You and I both know that doesn't work. Often the greatest way to avoid temptation is to avoid the situation that causes it. As Solomon says, "Watch the path of your feet" and "Turn your foot from evil." In other words, set the agenda by not allowing your feet to take you places you know you shouldn't go.

In short, how do you limit or reduce the stressors in your life caused by spiritual attack and temptation? You keep watch over your heart. Guard the real you. Do that first by understanding that you have an enemy and you're constantly under attack. Then set the agenda for each day by establishing boundaries for what you listen to, what you look at, and where you go.

There's no better pathway to experiencing God's unshakable, indescribable peace.

8

When Life Falls Apart

How Do I Keep God's Peace in Circumstances beyond My Control?

It's hard to imagine a more chaotic scene.

On July 16, 2018, a tour boat carrying dozens of passengers was struck by several "lava bombs" off the coast of Hawaii's Big Island. Lava bombs are created when magma flows into the ocean. As the molten rock comes in contact with the water, the reaction can be so intense that the lava literally explodes, sending burning chunks and shards thousands of feet through the air at high speeds.

That's what hit the tour boat, and the results were horrific. The rocks tore basketball-size chunks through the top of the boat and injured twenty-three people. One passenger suffered a fractured femur. Many others were taken to the hospital by ambulance once the boat limped back to shore.

There's some irony in that story. The tour boat was part of a company that offered lava tours—people paid money to go out on the boat and see the magma oozing into the ocean. According to the website, "Lava boat tours are an exciting way to experience the molten hot lava entering the sea. See, Hear and Feel the heat from your front row seat onboard one of our world class catamarans." The company promises its passengers "a life-changing experience."[1]

Beyond that single incident, the months-long eruption of the Kīlauea volcano has been one of the more explosive natural disasters of recent years. (Yes, pun intended.) I used to think volcanos always erupted from the top. That's what happens in movies, at least. What made the Kīlauea eruption so dangerous, though, was that the eruption proceeded from the sides. Not only that, but much of the eruption happened underground!

On May 3, 2018, the first fissure opened up on the southeast corner of the Big Island. Magma had traveled underground for miles and then burst out in the middle of a residential neighborhood, destroying dozens of homes. In the coming weeks, more than twenty additional fissures erupted. Altogether, the lava flow destroyed more than seven hundred homes, covered entire neighborhoods in molten rock, and added almost nine hundred acres of new land to the island.

You know what else I learned as I researched that event? Volcanic eruptions aren't always the most dangerous part of volcanic eruptions. Meaning, those eruptions can cause other disasters. For example, during the most active months of the Kīlauea eruption, the volcano itself and the area surrounding it experienced more than sixty thousand earthquakes. Not only that, but when the lava hit the ocean, it created a phenomenon called "laze"—as in a "lava haze." The mixture of magma and seawater creates hydrochloric acid and volcanic glass particles that are thrown into the air and can travel great distances. Exposure to this laze can seriously damage a person's eyes, skin, and lungs.[2]

I paid attention to the Kīlauea volcanic eruption because I saw it as one more reminder of how huge and powerful the world can be. It's also another reminder of how small and weak we are as human beings in the grand scheme of things. We like to think we can control everything around us—even the world in which we live. But every so often something happens that shows us how quickly we can be thrown into circumstances well beyond our control.

That's what I want to focus on in our final chapter together.

Specifically, much of what we've covered in recent chapters has applied to circumstances within our control. We've seen how to remove stressors from our schedules, our finances, our relationships, our decisions, and even attacks from our enemies. By doing what we can to remove stressors in these areas, we reduce the amount of stress in our lives and open ourselves more fully to experience God's peace.

But what about circumstances in which we have no control? How do we maintain a stressless life when it seems like everything around us is falling apart? The answer begins with a shift in focus.

A Shift in Focus

Many different factors can cause us to feel out of control in our lives. Some of those factors are global in scale, such as pandemics, economic recessions, wars and other forms of strife, natural disasters, and so on. Others are more limited to our individual lives, such as job loss, health problems, divorce, mental illness, spiritual struggles, and more.

Whatever the cause, the way we handle ourselves when circumstances get out of control—including the amount of stress we endure—is directly connected to our focus in those moments. When we focus on the right things, we can maintain a sense of peace. When we focus on the wrong things, we become more and more stressed.

Unfortunately, most of us focus on the wrong things during difficult circumstances. Specifically, we either look out or we look in, when we should be looking up.

To look out is to focus on the circumstances around us that are spinning out of control. It means focusing our attention on the medical bills that keep piling up. Or the growing list of companies that don't respond to our résumé. Or the number of people who have died from the latest virus. Looking out means keeping our focus on the problem.

The danger with looking out is that it makes us more and more aware of what's wrong while preventing us from finding a solution. It keeps our sights on our circumstances.

The other way many people react to circumstances beyond their control is to look in, meaning they focus on themselves. What they're feeling. How they're being affected. And what they're going to do to regain some control.

The danger of having that focus, of course, is that usually there's nothing we can do to regain control. Remember our definition of *stress* from the beginning of this book? *Stress* is "fearful concern experienced when life's demands seem greater than my ability to meet them." Well, if we respond to difficult circumstances by focusing on ourselves, all we're going to do is become more and more aware that we don't have the resources to make things better and that the demands of our circumstances are greater than our ability to manage.

Which means we're just going to experience more and more stress.

So then, what's the right focus to have when circumstances have gone beyond your control? The answer is to look up. To focus not on the circumstance and not on ourselves but on God. The answer is to focus on the One who does have the necessary resources to solve the problem—the One who also happens to be able to fill us with peace no matter what circumstances we experience.

There's a great picture of these different focuses in the Gospel of Mark:

> After dismissing the crowd, they took Him along with them in the boat, just as He was; and other boats were with Him. And a fierce gale of wind developed, and the waves were breaking over the boat so much that the boat was already filling with water. And yet Jesus Himself was in the stern, asleep on the cushion; and they woke Him and said to Him, "Teacher, do You not care that we are perishing?" And He got up and rebuked the wind and said to the sea, "Hush, be still." And the wind died down and it became perfectly calm. And He said to them, "Why are you afraid? Do you still have no faith?" They became very much afraid and said to one another, "Who, then, is this, that even the wind and the sea obey Him?" (4:36–41)

It's not mentioned specifically here, but I know some of the disciples in that boat were focused on the storm. Several of them were professional fishermen, so I'm certain once they understood they were facing more than a regular storm, they got to work. They tried their best to row or bail or do whatever they could to fix the situation in their own strength. They were looking out.

Other disciples were looking in. They woke up Jesus and said, "Do You not care that we are perishing?" (v. 38), meaning "Can't You see how this situation is affecting me?" They were looking in.

Jesus rebuked them because He wanted to change their focus. "Why are you afraid? Do you still have no faith?" (v. 40). He wanted them to recognize who was in the boat with them. He wanted them to look up and see that if Jesus was sleeping peacefully, they could take comfort in His peace. Because the situation was under control.

Here's the key principle that serves as the foundation for everything we're going to explore in this chapter: *our circumstances do not shape the way we view our God; our God shapes the way we view our circumstances.*

I know that principle can be a source of hope in your life, even in the most difficult of circumstances. Because as you'll see over these next few pages, God is active, God is sovereign, and God is personal. And because those things are true, you can have peace when circumstances seem out of control.

God Is Active

There's a verse of Scripture from the Old Testament that God has used on multiple occasions to change my perspective and shift my focus when life seemed out of control. Here it is from the book of Amos:

> For behold, He who forms mountains and creates
>   the wind,
> And declares to a person what are His thoughts,
> He who makes dawn into darkness
> And treads on the high places of the earth,
> The LORD God of armies is His name. (4:13)

I love that verse! What a rock for us to run to and jump on in the midst of shifting circumstances. This verse is packed with truths about God's nature, and the first truth I want to highlight is that God is active.

Many people in our culture seem to believe that God is distant. That He is passive. That He is sitting on the sidelines of the universe, completely uninterested in what happens. These people picture God as a divine clockmaker who put together the gears of the universe, started them spinning, and then wandered off to focus on new projects.

> **Our circumstances do not shape the way we view our God; our God shapes the way we view our circumstances.**

I've noticed that even Jesus followers can drift into this way of thinking when they encounter circumstances beyond their control. During difficult times, it's easy to wonder if God might be taking a break or if He doesn't really care about us after all. It's easy to ask questions like, *Where is God right now? Why isn't He doing anything?*

Amos had something much different to say about God. And it's important to know that Amos wasn't writing to people who were doing great in life. No, Amos was writing to a nation experiencing famine, drought, persecution, and even a plague. In other words, Amos was writing to people smack in the middle of circumstances beyond their control.

Look again at what he writes in 4:13:

> For behold, He who forms mountains and creates
>   the wind,
> And declares to a person what are His thoughts,
> He who makes dawn into darkness
> And treads on the high places of the earth,
> The LORD God of armies is His name.

Notice there are five verbs in that passage that describe God's activity in our world: *forms*, *creates*, *declares*, *makes*, and *treads*. Amos is highlighting a God who is active within His creation. It's also interesting that each of those terms was recorded as a participle in the original Hebrew language. That's important because participles are ongoing. They don't just describe something God did or does; they describe who He is continuously.

I like the way Jesus described God's activity in our world. "My Father is always working," He said, "and so am I" (John 5:17 NLT). To understand that, I like to think about my heart. Yours too. Have you noticed that your heart has never taken a minute to rest? Not once. From the first moment it was formed while you were in your mother's womb until right this second, your heart has contracted and released, contracted and released, contracted and released. It never stops beating. It never stops working—just like God.

If we take a closer look at the five verbs mentioned above, we see that God's activity in our world is powerful. The words *forms* and *creates* are translated from the same Hebrew terms used to describe the power of God's creation in Genesis 1 and 2. God is omnipotent—and He is all-powerful—and every action He takes is born out of that power.

We also see that God's activity is wise. In the original language, that word translated "declares" speaks to that which is unknown being made known and understood. It's a form of revelation. God is active in our world, and He reveals things to us we wouldn't otherwise be able to know. God is omniscient (all-knowing), and His every action is rooted in His deep and eternal wisdom.

Finally, God's activity is present. It's close. When Amos 4:13 declares that God "treads on the high places," the prophet is speaking to the omnipresence of God—to the truth that God is everywhere at all times. We never have to face any circumstance by ourselves, because wherever we are and whatever we're going through, God is right there with us. He is present.

The psalmist declares,

> God is our refuge and strength,
> A very ready help in trouble. (Ps. 46:1)

He understood that God is active in the world—and not just in the world as a general term, but God is active in our lives specifically. Your life and my life. He acts in power and wisdom, and He's present with us no matter what we endure.

Here's the reality: God is at work today. Right this moment. No matter what we're experiencing or what we face, we can be confident that God is at work. He's at work in our lives, He's at work in our families, and He's at work all over the world.

Therefore, we can hold on to His peace, even when our circumstances spin out of control.

God Is Sovereign

Not only is God constantly and continuously active in our world, but He is also sovereign. God is sovereign over all things, including our circumstances.

Now, *sovereign* is one of those words we like to use in church because it sounds cool. We throw it around all the time in sermons, songs, Bible studies, and more. But what does it actually mean? What am I saying when I declare that God is sovereign?

I went to onelook.com, which is one of my favorite reference websites because it offers close to fifty definitions for most words. According to the site, *sovereign* can mean "one who exercises supreme authority" or "a supreme ruler" or "supreme in rank or authority." Do you see the theme?

Eventually I wrote my own definition. According to the *Vance Pitman Dictionary*, to be sovereign is to be "the one who is large and in charge." That's sovereignty. That's really what the word means. And when it comes to the world we live in, only One is large and in charge: our God. He is sovereign.

Looking back at Amos 4:13, that verse reveals God's sovereignty in two ways. Speaking of God, the prophet writes, "For behold, He who forms mountains and creates the wind." Mountains and wind. Those two images represent two aspects of God's sovereignty.

First, "mountains" represent everything in our world that's stable and under control—everything that's certain. After all, what could be more stable and certain than a mountain?

Las Vegas is bordered by a mountain range, and we have one peak in particular, Mount Charleston, that is 11,916 feet in elevation. That makes it one of the top two hundred highest mountains in America. You can see Mount Charleston from all over the city and the surrounding suburbs—including from my house.

You know what I didn't do this morning? I didn't rush over to my window as soon as I woke up to check if Mount Charleston was still there. In fact, I've lived in Las Vegas for more than twenty years now—more than 7,500 days. And every single one of those days, I've been able to count on the reality of Mount Charleston standing watch over our city. Because it's stable. It's certain.

Lots of things in our world are similarly certain and stable. We can count on them. And the reason we can rely on these things isn't because they're reliable in and of themselves but because their builder and maintainer is our God who is large and in charge.

Now, maybe you're thinking, *That's great, Vance, but there's lots of stuff in my life that's very unstable and uncertain—especially when my circumstances are beyond my control!*

Good point. And that's why Amos mentions the wind. He talks about our God "who creates the wind." After all, what's more unpredictable than the wind? What's more uncertain? We don't know where it comes from, and we don't really have any way to tell where it's going. It's invisible and mysterious.

The wind is also powerful. That's a good thing when you've got the ability to harness that power, such as with a sailboat or a windmill. But the wind's power and unpredictability can also be a deadly combination.

Jason Nash knows better than most just how powerful and unpredictable the wind can be. When a huge storm with tornado warnings rolled across downtown Nashville in March 2020, many people were caught off guard and rushed to find shelter. Nobody was in a worse spot than Jason, though—he was 375 feet up in the air, in the cab of a construction crane! Unable to descend because of the wind speeds, Jason was forced to watch helplessly from his elevated perch as a funnel cloud formed and bore down on his location.

Thankfully, the tornado veered away in time, and Jason lived to talk about his adventure. (He was also able to reveal the videos he recorded of the tornado from almost four hundred feet in the air, which are wild!)[3]

Still, you and I understand that sometimes the storm doesn't veer away—both literally and figuratively. Sometimes we suffer a direct hit. Sometimes we find ourselves not just in circumstances beyond our control but in the midst of situations that bring suffering and pain. Even death. What then?

Amos wants us to know that even then, the God who created the wind is still large and in charge. He's sovereign over not only the stable and certain elements of our lives but also those we never saw coming—the things we didn't expect, the moments we couldn't prepare for, and even the situations that cause suffering and pain.

No matter what we're experiencing right now, and no matter how chaotic things may seem in the future, it's critical to understand that our circumstances did not catch God by surprise. Nor will our circumstances ever overwhelm His resources. That doesn't mean everything will be fine—that doesn't mean we won't endure hardship or pain. But it does mean we can remain connected to the One who's in control of all things.

Remember, our circumstances do not shape the way we view God; instead, God shapes the way we view our circumstances. As Paul writes, "[Jesus] is before all things, and in Him all things hold together" (Col. 1:17). That means before the first star ever appeared in the sky or the first ray of sunshine ever warmed a spot on the earth—before human existence began—there was a sovereign Designer. Our God spoke it all into existence, and Scripture says He's holding it all together so every single section of our world and our experience fits together as part of a whole that is His plan. His purpose.

When all is said and done, governments and political leaders aren't in charge. Educational institutions aren't in charge. Doctors and hospitals aren't in charge. Pastors and churches aren't in charge. Our God alone is large and in charge. He is sovereign. And therefore we can maintain our hold on His gift of peace when we focus on Him.

God Is Personal

When we find ourselves in circumstances beyond our control, the first thing we need to do is shift our focus away from ourselves and our circumstances so we can focus on God. That's because our God is active in this world, our God is sovereign over this world, and finally, our God is personal. He is present within our world.

Take another look at how Amos closes out verse 13 of chapter 4:

> For behold, He who forms mountains and creates
>   the wind,
> And declares to a person what are His thoughts,
> He who makes dawn into darkness
> And treads on the high places of the earth,
> *The* LORD *God of armies is His name.* (emphasis
>   added)

That means our active, sovereign God has a name—a name you and I can know. Do you know why God has a name? Because He is a Person. Our God is not some generic "force" hovering out in the universe. No, our God is a Person. He has a face and eyes that see you. He has hands that reach out to catch you and arms that are strong to hold you. He has feet that allow Him to walk with you and stand beside you. He has a heart that cares for you.

Our God is a Person, which means He's personally involved in not only the world generally but also your life specifically.

I love what Scripture says in Proverbs 18:10:

> The name of the LORD is a strong tower;
>   the righteous runs into it and is safe.

If you're a follower of Jesus, you don't have to be tossed back and forth by the winds and uncertainties of your circumstances. You can run to God, your strong tower, and be safe.

In the same way, if you've never met Jesus in a personal way, you have the opportunity to do so at any time—even right this moment. The Bible says, "For whoever will call on the name of the Lord will be saved" (Rom. 10:13 NASB1995). The word *whoever* in that verse doesn't mean whoever is good enough. It doesn't mean whoever is rich enough. It doesn't mean whoever has it all together and is worthy.

No, *whoever* means whoever. Anyone. Everyone. You.

As we've seen throughout these pages, life is a stress test. In fact, life is a series of stress tests, sometimes one on top of another. Each day, life throws more stressors at us and tries to pile them on our shoulders. Schedules, finances, relationships, decisions, spiritual attacks, difficult circumstances—we've only scratched the surface when it comes to all the hardships and stress life can throw our way. That's the bad news.

> Our God is a Person, which means He's personally involved in not only the world generally but also your life specifically.

The good news is that we can know this active, sovereign, personal God. We can call on His name. And when we do that—when we make Him the foundation of our lives and allow Jesus to live in us and through us—we can be filled with His peace.

Please remember that God's peace isn't far off or far away. It's not something we have to wait years to earn or achieve. It's available right now. Right this moment. Today.

When life piles stressors on our shoulders, we must resist the temptation to push back in our own strength. Resist the temptation to try to figure out what we're going to do about it. Doing so will only lead to fearful concern and awareness of our own inabilities—our own limits. In other words, it will only lead to stress.

Instead, choose to live a stressless life by looking to God and calling on His name. *Lord Jesus, my God and Savior, what will You do about this? What are You about to accomplish through this?* Choose to be filled with God's peace.

And as you experience that peace, I hope and pray you'll share it with others. In fact, I'm asking you to share it with others. The more you know the wonder of God's peace filling every moment of your everyday life, the more you should declare the goodness of that peace to anyone willing to listen.

Remember, I've come to understand these truths through experience. As I shared at the beginning of this book, I've learned these lessons the hard way. That's how I know they're true. That's how I've been filled with God's peace in every area of my everyday life, and I know the same can be true for you.

May God bless you and me, not only by helping us live free from the burden of stress but also by giving us the opportunity to change the world with the good news of His unshakable, indescribable peace.

Acknowledgments

Thanks be to God for His unshakable presence that allows me to experience His indescribable peace every moment of every day.

Thanks to my wife, Kristie, who has lovingly walked with me over every mountaintop and through every valley that life has brought our way. I would not have survived the opening story of this book without her in my life. Thanks, babe, for so loving Jesus and allowing Him to love so deeply through you!

Thanks to my kids, their spouses, and my grandchildren, whose lives bring me so much joy and at the same time have allowed me to test the principles of this book throughout the years. I love you all dearly!

Thanks to Sam O'Neal for his work with me on this project. Your unique ability to communicate through the written word is a gift to my life and the kingdom. Keep writing, my friend.

Thanks to the Hope Church family for understanding that, first and foremost, pastors are people. People who need to love Jesus and follow Him in a healthy way spiritually, mentally, emotionally, and physically. Thanks for giving priority to the health of your leaders and the families who love them.

Thanks to Travis Ogle for his partnership in the gospel for almost twenty years. Your strategic leadership and servant's spirit have allowed me to enjoy God's peace in incalculable ways. Thanks for lifting me up and holding me accountable through all the seasons and rhythms of life and ministry.

Thanks to Shagufta Brown for helping me organize my life in a way that allows me to write this book with honesty and integrity. Because of your careful attention to the details of my life and ministry, I am able to experience, not just aspire to, the promise of God's peace.

Thanks to Sealy Yates and the entire Yates & Yates team for your belief in me and the content of this book. Your advocacy and advice have brought God's peace into my life, time and time again.

Thanks to Brian Vos and the Baker team for all the work that happens behind the scenes to allow projects like this to come to fruition. Your contribution to the kingdom is bearing fruit into eternity.

Finally, thanks to all those who have served on Hope Church's Stewardship Team through the years. Your investment in this church, my life, and the lives of the pastors of this fellowship has allowed us to experience God's peace in ways that are truly beyond description—the peace of God that surpasses all comprehension!

Notes

Introduction

1. Eric Patterson, LPC, "Stress Facts and Statistics," The Recovery Village, November 6, 2020, https://www.therecoveryvillage.com/mental -health/stress/related/stress-statistics/.

2. Patterson, "Stress Facts and Statistics."

3. "2020 Data Charts," American Psychological Association, accessed June 7, 2021, https://www.apa.org/news/press/releases/stress/2020/info graphics-october.

Chapter 1 Anxious Living

1. Penn State Football, "A message from Journey Brown: I can still remember the first time I truly fell in love with the game I've been playing since 4th grade. Back then it was a game," Facebook, November 11, 2020, https://m.facebook.com/PSUFball/photos/pb.90410823197.-2207520000 ../10157983862623198/?type=3&source=43.

2. Mark Wogenrich, "'It's Heartbreaking': Journey Brown Retires from Football Because of Heart Condition," *Sports Illustrated*, November 11, 2020, https://www.si.com/college/pennstate/college/pennstate/foot ball/penn-state-running-back-journey-brown.

3. Dictionary.com, s.v. "stress," accessed May 24, 2021, https://www .dictionary.com/browse/stress?s=t.

4. CBS Interactive Staff, "The Most Venomous Animals on Earth, Ranked," CNET, April 29, 2016, https://www.cnet.com/pictures/the-most -venomous-animals-on-earth-ranked/.

5. Albert Barnes, *Notes on the New Testament: Ephesians, Philippians, Colossians*, ed. Robert Frew (London: Blackie & Son, 1983), 214. Accessed via Logos, July 6, 2021.

6. "The Effects of Stress on Your Body," WebMD, December 14, 2019, https://www.webmd.com/balance/stress-management/effects-of-stress-on-your-body.

7. Deborah S. Hartz-Seeley, "Chronic Stress Is Linked to the Six Leading Causes of Death," *Miami Herald*, March 21, 2014, https://www.miamiherald.com/living/article1961770.html.

8. Mayo Clinic Staff, "Stress Symptoms: Effects on Your Body and Behavior," Mayo Clinic, April 4, 2019, https://www.mayoclinic.org/healthy-lifestyle/stress-management/in-depth/stress-symptoms/art-20050987.

9. Clyde Cranford, *Because We Love Him: Embracing a Life of Holiness* (Colorado Springs: Multnomah, 2002), 240.

10. A. W. Tozer, *The Knowledge of the Holy* (New York: HarperCollins, 1978), 1.

11. Matt Chandler, "Don't Waste Your Cancer: An Interview with Matt Chandler," Ligonier Ministries, July 1, 2011, https://www.ligonier.org/learn/articles/dont-waste-your-cancer-interview-matt-chandler/.

Chapter 2 Abundant Life

1. Kristen Zambo, "Calvin Carter Sentenced to Four Life Terms Plus 280 Years for Quadruple Murder," *Rockford Register Star*, September 8, 2017, https://www.rrstar.com/news/20170908/calvin-carter-sentenced-to-four-life-terms-plus-280-years-for-quadruple-murder.

2. Zambo, "Calvin Carter Sentenced."

3. Andrea V. Watson, "Rockford Quadruple Homicide Victim's Mother Finds Peace in Forgiveness," *Rockford Register Star*, December 26, 2020, https://www.rrstar.com/story/news/2020/12/26/rockford-quadruple-homicide-victims-mother-finds-peace-forgiveness/4028050001/.

4. Watson, "Rockford Quadruple Homicide."

5. Watson, "Rockford Quadruple Homicide."

6. Cranford, *Because We Love Him*, 241.

Chapter 3 Running Out of Time

1. Guinness World Records Staff, "Incredible Records That Were YouTube Hits in 2020," Guinness World Records, December 21, 2020, https://www.guinnessworldrecords.com/news/2020/12/incredible-records-that-were-youtube-hits-in-2020-643387.

2. Henry T. Blackaby and Claude V. King, *Experiencing God: Knowing and Doing the Will of God* (Nashville: Lifeway, 1990), 45.

3. Adrian Rogers' Daily Devotionals, "Would You Like a Second Chance?—Love Worth Finding—December 31," CrossWalk.com, December 31, 2019, https://www.crosswalk.com/devotionals/loveworthfinding/love-worth-finding-december-31-2019.html.

Chapter 4 Making Ends Meet

1. "Firefighter Waiting on Coronavirus Stimulus Check Sees $8 Million in Bank Account," ClickOrlando.com, April 14, 2020, https://www.click orlando.com/news/local/2020/04/14/firefighter-waiting-on-coronavirus-stimulus-check-sees-8-million-in-bank-account/.

2. "Stress in America 2020," American Psychological Association, October 2020, https://www.apa.org/news/press/releases/stress/2020/report-october.

3. Statista Research Department, "Percentage Distribution of Household Income in the US in 2019," Statista, January 20, 2021, https://www.statista .com/statistics/203183/percentage-distribution-of-household-income-in-the-us/.

4. Jeffrey Dew, Sonya Britt, and Sandra Huston, "Examining the Relationship between Financial Issues and Divorce," School of Family Studies and Human Services, Kansas State University, September 4, 2012, https://onlinelibrary.wiley.com/doi/abs/10.1111/j.1741-3729.2012.00715.x.

5. Melissa J. Murphy, "Financial Stress and Its Effect on Children," Next Generation Parenting, May 25, 2018, http://www.nextgeneration parenting.org/parenting_focus/financial-stress-and-its-effect-on-children.

6. Gregg Easterbrook, "The Real Truth about Money," *Time*, January 17, 2005, http://content.time.com/time/magazine/article/0,9171,1015883,00.html.

7. Randy Alcorn, *The Treasure Principle: Discovering the Secret of Joyful Giving* (Sisters, OR: Multnomah, 2001), 61–65.

8. "Study: Average American's Savings Account Balance is $3,500," The Ascent, September 10, 2020, https://www.fool.com/the-ascent/research /average-savings-account-balance/.

9. "Survey: 65% of Americans Have No Idea How Much They Spent Last Month," Intuit Mint Life, May 29, 2020, https://mint.intuit.com /blog/budgeting/spending-knowledge-survey/.

Chapter 5 Dealing with People

1. Julia Naftulin, "A Couple Celebrating Their 70-year Wedding Anniversary Share Their Tips for Relationship Success, From Dinner Dates

to Hobbies," Insider, July 15, 2020, https://www.insider.com/couple
-married-70-years-advice-for-relationship-success-2020-7.

2. Naftulin, "A Couple Celebrating."

3. Naftulin, "A Couple Celebrating."

4. Naftulin, "A Couple Celebrating."

5. Naftulin, "A Couple Celebrating."

6. American Psychological Association, *Stress in America 2015: Paying with Our Health*, report released February 4, 2015, https://www.apa.org/news/press/releases/stress/2014/stress-report.pdf.

7. Roy Hession, *The Calvary Road* (Winslow, England: Rickfords Hill, 2013), 39–40.

8. Hession, *The Calvary Road*, 23.

9. Security.org Team, "Survey: Nearly 4 in 10 People Have Had Packages Stolen," Security.org, October 17, 2019, https://www.security.org/resources/stolen-packages-survey/.

10. Katie Schoolov, "With Package Theft at an All-Time High, Amazon and Others Are Fighting Back," CNBC, January 11, 2020, https://www.cnbc.com/2020/01/10/package-theft-how-amazon-google-others-are-fighting-porch-pirates.html.

11. Jeremy Rehm, "The Four Fundamental Forces of Nature," Space.com, October 1, 2019, https://www.space.com/four-fundamental-forces.html.

12. Roy Hession, *My Calvary Road* (Fort Washington, PA: CLC Publications, 2011), 14.

Chapter 6 Choices, Choices

1. Madison Park, Keith Allen, Lawrence Davidson, and Liz Turrell, "Hawaii False Missile Alert 'Button Pusher' Is Fired," CNN, January 30, 2018, https://www.cnn.com/2018/01/30/us/hawaii-false-alarm-investigation/index.html.

2. Warren Wiersbe, *The Wiersbe Bible Commentary: Old Testament* (Colorado Springs: David C. Cook, 2007), 1054.

3. Charles F. Stanley, *Charles Stanley's Handbook for Christian Living: Biblical Answers to Life's Tough Questions* (Nashville: Thomas Nelson, 2008), 407.

4. Wiersbe, *The Wiersbe Bible Commentary*, 1097.

Chapter 7 Guard Your Heart

1. Bob Barber, "10 People of the Second Millennium," *Rensselaer Republican*, May 1, 2006, https://www.newsbug.info/rensselaer_republican

/news/10-people-of-the-second-millennium/article_bcea8644-a9a3-5e30 -89aa-a9af4d3f333f.html.

2. Dan Elliot, "Things to Know: 'The Most Secure Facility in the World,'" Associated Press, May 12, 2018, https://apnews.com/article /37e32892f43c41ef98bcc2991b52756d.

3. Arizona Christian University Cultural Research Center, "American Worldview Inventory 2020—At a Glance," news release no. 3, April 21, 2020, https://www.arizonachristian.edu/wp-content/uploads/2020/04 /CRC-AWVI-2020-Release-03_Perceptions-of-God.pdf.

4. John MacArthur Jr., *The MacArthur New Testament Commentary: Ephesians* (Chicago: Moody, 1986), 341.

5. Caleb Moore, "Pornography and Christians," *Baptist Messenger*, March 11, 2020, https://www.baptistmessenger.com/pornography-and -christians/.

6. Kelly Burch, "How Social Media Affects the Mental Health of Teen- agers," Insider.com, March 16, 2020, https://www.insider.com/how-does -social-media-affect-teenagers.

7. *Pornography and Public Health Research Summary* (Washington, DC: National Center on Sexual Exploitation, 2019), 1, https://familywatch .org/wp-content/uploads/sites/5/2019/07/NCOSE_Pornography-Public -Health_RESEARCH-SUMMARY_8-15-17.pdf.

8. Burch, "How Social Media Affects."

Chapter 8 When Life Falls Apart

1. Doyle Rice, "At Least 23 Injured as 'Lava Bomb' Hits Tour Boat Near Hawaii's Kilauea Volcano," *USA Today*, July 16, 2018, https:// www.usatoday.com/story/news/nation/2018/07/16/hawaii-volcano-least -12-injured-lava-bomb-hits-tourist-boat/789467002/.

2. Cox Media Group, "Kilauea Eruption: As Many As 700 Homes De- stroyed on Hawaii's Big Island," *Atlanta-Journal Constitution*, June 12, 2018, https://www.ajc.com/news/national/explosive-eruption-reported -kilauea-summit-hawaii/hN3465a4OowMiJPHGOlMEP/.

3. "Crane Operator Rides Out Tornado Nearly 400 Feet above Down- town Nashville," *Tennessean*, March 5, 2020, https://www.tennessean .com/story/news/local/2020/03/05/nashville-crane-operator-tornado -video/4961931002/.

About the Author

Vance Pitman is the senior pastor of Hope Church, a community of believers in Las Vegas, Nevada, focused on the mission of connecting people to live the life of a Jesus follower. God gave Vance both a passion for God's kingdom and a vision to launch a church focused on joining in God's eternal, redemptive mission of making disciples and multiplying the church among every tribe, tongue, people, and nation. Having launched Hope Church in 2001 from a small group of eighteen adults in a living room, Vance now shepherds a multiethnic fellowship of thousands of members that has planted dozens of churches in the western United States. He is also a national mobilizer for the North American Mission Board (NAMB), a member of the Ethics and Religious Liberty Commission (ERLC) Leadership Council, and a national resource leader for the 6:4 Fellowship. Besides *The Stressless Life: Experiencing the Unshakable Presence of God's Indescribable Peace*, Vance is also the author of *Unburdened: Stop Living for Jesus So Jesus Can Live Through You*. He and his wife, Kristie, live in Henderson, Nevada, and have four children and two grandchildren.

Find Freedom from the
Burden of Religion

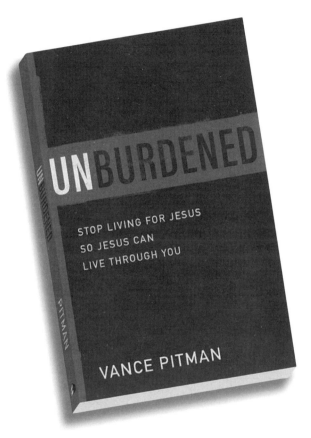

In *Unburdened*, Vance closely examines the life of Jesus in the Gospels to reveal the soul-awakening truths that have set him and many others free from the burden of religion. With raw honesty and real-life applications, he helps readers escape the exasperating cycle of trying to live for Jesus and shows them instead the power of discovering the joy of a love relationship with Jesus.

Tune in to Pastor Vance's
LEADERSHIP PODCAST

A conversation all about leadership, vision, and joining in God's activity wherever you are.

Find episodes at **VancePitman.com** or on your favorite podcasting app.

CONNECT WITH VANCE

 vancepitman

 vancepitman

 VancePitmanLV

VancePitman.com

Find out more about
HOPE CHURCH

VISIT HopeChurchLV.com